Hopes
and
Fears
Working with Today's Independent School Parents

Robert Evans and Michael Thompson

National Association
of Independent Schools

© 2021 by the National Association of Independent Schools

ISBN: 978-1-63115-043-2
Printed in the United States of America

National Association
of Independent Schools

As the largest association of independent schools, the National Association of Independent Schools (NAIS) co-creates the future of education by uniting and empowering our community. NAIS provides services to more than 1,900 schools and associations of schools in the United States and abroad, including more than 1,600 nonprofit, private K-12 schools in the U.S. that are self-determining in mission and program and are governed by independent boards.

For more information, go to the NAIS website at http://www.nais.org.

Editors: Susan Hunt, Myra McGovern, Karla Taylor
Design: Fletcher Design, Inc./Washington, DC
Cover image: Damircudic/Getty Images

CONTENTS

Acknowledgments

We want to thank the hundreds of teachers and administrators who have, over the last 20 years, shared with us their challenges and successes in working with independent school parents. We would also like to thank the hundreds of parents who have trusted us with stories of figuring out their children and dealing with their children's schools. Though we can't begin to name all these good people, we simply could not have written this book without the willingness of so many to share their hopes and fears with us.

While writing, we relied on the wisdom and experience of many educators who were good enough to let us interview them or to read the book at various stages and share their recommendations: Kai Bynum, Tim Carr, Drew Casertano, Norman Colb, Randall Dunn, Robert Greene, Cathy Hall, Rachel Jean-Baptiste, Jerry Katz, Lucinda Lee Katz, Rick Melvoin, Tom Northrup, Bill Polk, Mark Segar, Keith Shahan, Bruce Shaw, Robert Smith, Howard Stevenson, and the Vorenbergs: Amy, Tom, and Ella. Michael's literary agent, Gail Ross, provided us with helpful counsel and advice.

We extend warm appreciation to NAIS President Donna Orem for the deep support she brought to this book from its inception. For their thorough, thoughtful input, we owe thanks to our NAIS editors: Myra McGovern, Caroline Blackwell, and Susan Hunt. And we want to give special recognition to Karla Taylor at NAIS: She won our trust and took the manuscript under her editor's wing, seeing it to a happy conclusion.

The book is better for the efforts of all. Its flaws, of course, remain ours.

■

This book aspires to help teachers and administrators understand the sources of, and cope constructively with, the changing landscape of the parent-school relationship.

Introduction

Independent schools only exist because of the hopes and fears of parents. Parents are willing to pay expensive tuitions because they hope that the school will maximize their children's learning. They hope their children will experience better and more supportive teaching, smaller class sizes, more opportunities to play on a varsity team or get a role in the school musical, and perhaps more experienced college counseling than they would in the larger local public school.

Independent schools also reassure parents that their children will be kept safe, that they will be known and loved, that they will make both friends and steady progress. When those things don't happen, parents can get scared and upset pretty quickly.

If independent schools exist because of parental hopes and fears, they run every day on the hopes and fears of teachers. Teachers who are drawn to work in independent education hope that their teaching will make a real difference in the lives of children; they want their teaching to be original, meaningful, even joyful. They hope not to be burdened by the bureaucracy, restrictions, and social problems of public schools. They also want their teaching to be respected and appreciated because they are trying hard to fulfill the expectations of parents and their children. When parents turn critical, teachers can get defensive and frightened pretty quickly.

In this book we address the inevitable collisions between the hopes and fears of parents and those of teachers. When teachers prepare for the profession of education, they may find out a great deal about the learning process itself, about curriculum, about classroom management, even about child development. But they may learn little or nothing about how to engage with parents or, more important, how to manage conflict with them.

Our goal is to help close this gap.

We are two psychologists who have each spent more than 50 years in schools. We both started out as classroom teachers, Rob as a high school English teacher who then did a brief stint as a preschool teacher; Michael as a middle school social studies teacher and later as a high school teacher-counselor. Separately, we each made the decision to leave our classrooms and get our doctorates in psychology, but we found we couldn't leave schools behind. We each have always had one foot in the world of clinical psychology and the other in education. Over the last 40 years, we have visited and consulted with more than 2,000 schools: independent, public, and international.

Since the late 1990s, much of our work has been to conduct professional development workshops for teachers, leadership trainings for administrators, talks on child development for parents, and retreats for boards of trustees. We've each consulted regularly (weekly, monthly) over a period of many years at particular schools, coming to know them intimately. And we've also done lots of crisis intervention. We've visited schools after tragedies and blowups (a sudden death, the firing of a beloved head of school, a suicide, a sexual misconduct scandal, a schism on the board, even several murders) and after national disasters like 9/11, the financial meltdown of 2008, and, more recently, COVID-19. We *know* schools, particularly independent schools.

However, any wisdom we have to share doesn't come just from being school consultants. As boys, we each attended independent schools. We watched how *our* parents dealt with our schools. When we became parents, we both sent our children to independent schools in the Boston area; more recently, as grandparents, we have watched our grandchildren attend independent schools in far-flung states. We have winced as we wrote out large tuition checks; we have cheered our children's and grandchildren's progress in their schools; and we have suffered during the times they were lonely and discouraged learners. And, yes, we have sometimes been angry—very angry—when we felt they were not being seen or being taught well.

One of the things we know about independent schools is that the majority of their relationships with parents go well. Most independent school parents are satisfied customers. Their children are excited to go to school, love their friends, and seem to be learning in an enriched environment that brings out many aspects of their personalities. Their day-to-day experience usually confirms the tuition value proposition for their parents.

When we ask teachers whether the vast majority of parents in their school are good people who send good children, they answer yes. Most parents love their child's school, and most teachers really like the majority of the parents. You can see the mutual respect and appreciation on display at graduation when teachers and parents are offering heartfelt thanks to one another.

If that were the whole story, we wouldn't have written this book. But it's not. Our work has given us a deep appreciation not just for the successes independent schools achieve but also for the challenges they face. Over the past 20 years, the most prominent of these challenges, by far, has been the relentless rise in educators' frustration in dealing with parents: parents' worries, their demands, their entire approach to their child's schooling. Repeatedly in our work in schools, conversations that begin in another topic area—governance, say, or middle school social cruelty—end up turning to parent behavior. More and more, schools ask us to speak with administrators about parent management, to conduct workshops on "Dealing with Difficult Parents" for faculties, and to present to parents themselves. We hope to help teachers and administrators understand the sources of, and cope constructively with, the changing landscape of the parent-school relationship.

Independent school parents vary widely in terms of socioeconomic status, religion, race, ethnicity, sexual orientation, and many other cultural identifiers. In this book, we will concentrate mostly on the parents who present by far the greatest number of challenges to the school: those who pay full tuition. They constitute the majority of the parent body in nearly every independent school, and they are the parents on whom the schools most depend financially. They are often ambitious for their children and—above all—anxious *about* their children. They have big dreams, and they want their children to have a leg up. Many full-pay parents, however well-off, are, on average, much less confident about their children's future than they wish to be and much more concerned that their children's schooling provide sustained success and minimal frustration and disappointment.

Of course, full-pay parents aren't the only ones who have dreams. Parents of modest means know that their children who receive need-based financial aid (at least 25% of independent school students do[1]) might encounter income inequalities on a daily basis, but they want them in schools where teachers can really connect with them and nurture their potential.

Most of the parents we describe in this book are white. But one-third of the students attending NAIS schools are students of color.[2] Their parents are willing to risk sending them to a majority-white school where they might experience racial stress because the parents want their children to reap the benefits outlined above and have a future full of opportunity.

Teaching attracts people with a strong service ethic and a strong security orientation. For people with high levels of schooling, educators accept comparatively low compensation in exchange for the opportunity to educate children and for stability and autonomy; schools rarely dismiss teachers and typically grant them great freedom in their teaching. But above all, many teachers are conflict-avoidant. Indeed, conflict avoidance is a way of life in schools. Teachers are people who choose to spend their days with children and adolescents, something virtually no other adult, even the most loving parent, would willingly do. They thrive on this contact. Most are hardwired to accentuate the positive. Consequently, dealing with parents who are aggressive or critical is almost never in a teacher's wheelhouse. Administrators, who end up having to handle the toughest, most trying parents, often develop conflict management skills, but many still tend to delay confrontation as long as possible. Ultimately, to be successful in the independent school setting, every educator has to come to terms with difficult parents. We hope this book will help them do so.

THE PLAN OF THE BOOK

This book is organized into three parts.

Part 1: The Rising Tide of Anxiety explores the context underlying the dilemmas that parents pose for schools. In our experience, most of the difficult situations that parents present stem from a broadening and deepening anxiety about raising their children. This isn't true in all situations—especially not some of the most confrontational—but Part 1 details the sources of the sustained increase in parental anxiety.

Chapter 1 describes the inevitable tensions that are baked into the relationship between parents and teachers. These tensions have always existed and arise from normal forces: the intense love parents feel for their children; the knowledge that teachers acquire, and the attachment they develop, when teaching those same children; and the status difference between parents-as-customers and teachers-as-providers.[3]

Chapters 2 and 3 examine ways that child development contributes to parental anxiety and tension with teachers. Children, as they grow, are a moving target, frequently throwing their parents off-balance, and their developmental changes can become flashpoints between parents and schools. **Chapter 2** focuses on parents of lower school students and **Chapter 3** on parents of middle and upper school students.

Chapter 4 turns to two major non-school factors that have been intensifying parents' anxiety: accelerating social, economic, and technological change that makes it harder for parents to envision a safe, successful future for their children; and an epidemic of poor parenting advice that exaggerates both their expectations for, and worries about, their children.

Part 2: Challenges examines key dilemmas schools encounter in their actual dealings with parents.

Chapter 5 provides a deeper look into the psychology of parents. We draw a fundamental distinction between the vast majority, who can be worked with (we call them "95 percenters"), and the small minority ("5 percenters"), who often have personality and other disorders that incline them to violate the school's behavioral norms and boundaries. The 5 percenters behave in ways that disrupt the school community and cause anxiety, fear, and frustration in teachers.

Chapter 6 turns to the issues that can arise between Black parents and white educators. These issues do not have to do with difficult behavior by Black parents but with the complexities and tensions often exacerbated by cultural differences, implicit biases, and assumptions.

Chapter 7 focuses on what schools should stop doing. It looks at the ways schools have traditionally tried to handle relationships with parents and argues that these methods are flawed and ineffective.

Part 3: Coping offers practical suggestions for resolving and preventing communication problems with parents. We recommend structural measures that educators can take at the institutional, schoolwide level and situational steps to take at the individual level to resolve differences and conflicts.

Chapter 8 makes the case for restructuring the home-school partnership into one in which the school acts as the senior partner. As the senior partner, the school clarifies expectations, roles, and responsibilities for all participants in the school—including parents—and is explicit about the minimum conditions of membership in the community.

Chapters 9 and 10 delve into the nitty-gritty of difficult encounters. *Chapter 9* presents a basic problem-solving toolkit, a set of straightforward measures that can help teachers and administrators improve connection and settle conflicts with the 95 percenters. *Chapter 10* provides an advanced toolkit for managing worst-case scenarios—the ones involving 5 percenter parents, including those who become toxic to the school community.

Finally, *Chapter 11* outlines ways administrators and heads of school can reduce and prevent serious communication problems with parents by training and supporting teachers.

ON BEHALF OF CHILDREN

Because this book's goal is to help educators at all levels enhance their repertoire of skills in working with parents, there may be times when students recede into the background, seeming almost forgotten as we hash out the tensions of the adult world. But even when we delve deeply into the interactions between schools and parents, we never forget the central mission that motivates us all: to educate children. We believe that children of all ages thrive when the adults in their lives get along better with each other and when they see the child in the same way.

As psychologists who have worked with many unhappy and divorced families, we know that all children devoutly wish for their parents to agree more, to not fight, and to get along better, so the kids can just play and grow and go to school in peace.

The very same logic applies to parents and teachers. If they can agree more and fight less, if they can view the child in the same way, then all the student has to do is go to school and learn. The key to forging and sustaining a strong alliance with parents is to understand their hopes and fears. In turn, this will help educators manage their own hopes and fears, and it will help all the adults collaborate on behalf of the children.

Portions of Chapters 7, 8, and 9 originally appeared, in different form, in Robert Evans' *Family Matters: How Schools Can Cope with the Crisis in Childrearing* (Jossey-Bass, 2004) and "Getting to No: Building True Collegiality in Schools" (*Independent School* magazine, Winter 2012).

Examples from heads of school and other administrators come from personal interviews with the authors. Other examples concerning parents and children come from the authors' consulting experiences. Names and details have been changed to ensure anonymity. Except where obvious or specifically indicated, from here on, "schools" refers to independent schools.

ENDNOTES

[1] NAIS, Data and Analysis for School Leadership (DASL), "Facts at a Glance: Year(s) 2019-20: Comparison as Group(s): All NAIS Member Schools"; online at https://www.nais.org/getmedia/cb3cbc7a-a703-43b9-9091-3680b66c782c/2019-20-Facts-at-a-Glance-(NAIS-Members).pdf.

[2] Ibid.

[3] NAIS has conducted extensive research about parents as "customers" in its Jobs-to-Be-Done work. NAIS has also researched the reasons that teachers choose to work in independent schools. These studies are available to NAIS members at nais.org/jtbdparents and nais.org/jtbdteachers.

PART 1

THE RISING TIDE OF ANXIETY

Several factors intensify the dilemmas families and schools face: The normal, inevitable tensions between parents and teachers. The developmental challenges children present. Accelerating social, economic, and technological change. And an epidemic of poor parenting advice.

■

Both parents and teachers want what's best for the student, but their different roles and perspectives can cause them to disagree about precisely what *is* best.

Chapter 1

Normal Tensions

Many parents and teachers describe their independent school as being "like a family," a heartwarming image meant to suggest affection, harmony, and safety. For psychologists, the image evokes a more complicated reaction. Every family is a dense, ambivalent knot of love, yearning, intimacy, worry, anger, struggle, and conflict. These are normal, inevitable tensions. They exist in the school "family," too, though they are rarely acknowledged publicly. This chapter examines the normal tensions between parents and educators that are found in every school.

Although no organization goes as deep into our hearts as family and none can cause the hurt that a family can, schools definitely stir strong feelings, too. Parents routinely say, "Our daughter loves her school," or "We love our son's school." And every parent sooner or later gets angry at the school, whether for small things—like lost coats and unexpected schedule changes—or big things—like bullying. Because our children are involved, schools often tap into our deepest feelings of love, hope, protectiveness, and disappointment. It begins at the first moment a parent drops a child off at school. Many pre-K or kindergarten parents have difficulty letting go of the child's hand at the classroom door on the first day.

Some go into the classroom to help their children put coats and backpacks in cubbies. Often, a parent will kneel down to hug the child and finally race out of the room, overwhelmed with feelings. Sometimes, a parent cannot bear to leave and sits down to stay awhile. If the parent is still there at lunchtime, the teacher may be thinking, "Uh-oh."

Taking a young child to school for the first time arouses some of the deepest concerns a parent can feel: Will my child be safe when not with me, when with strangers? Teachers inevitably become the focus for these fears, and they, in turn, experience their own worries: Will the parent trust me? Will I be able to connect with and teach this child to the parent's satisfaction?

None of this gets mentioned on the first day of school or at back-to-school night. But these and other fears underlie the home-school relationship and are easily aroused. In our experience, parents are prone to four natural fears that cause them to question their child's teacher (and the administrators who hire and supervise the teacher). And all teachers, in their interactions with parents, are prone to three natural fears, most of which mirror parents'.

These fears are no one's fault, nor can they be permanently fixed. They are baked into these relationships—just as conflicts and fears are baked into family relationships. For the most part, they subside quickly because most parents are trusting and most teachers are professional. However, they inevitably surge up in disruptive ways from time to time. Let's start by examining the parents' fears.

FOUR FEARS OF PARENTS

Not all parents voice all these concerns in so many words, but explicitly or implicitly, they have come up repeatedly in the hundreds of parent talks we've each conducted in schools over the years. They are all part of being human.

Parent Fear 1: Will my child be safe?

Humans, like all mammals, are biologically programmed to be ferociously protective of their young. The safety of our children is paramount; we would sacrifice our lives for them, just as a grizzly bear mother does when she charges a much larger male to protect her cubs. NAIS research on parent motivations tells us that one of the top reasons parents choose an independent school is that they want a structured, safe learning environment that will challenge their children academically and help them mature.[1]

Physical safety is part of this, but psychological safety is a key part of it, too. Parents want a place where their child will be well-treated and be able to learn. But children are vulnerable to slights, insults, and power plays by peers. All students come home at one time or another complaining about mistreatment by classmates. In addition, children sometimes misunderstand what adults say to them; they can get their feelings hurt by a teacher's brusque remark. They come home and say, "My teacher doesn't like me."

A child's complaints can inflame the grizzly bear protectiveness in parents. Parents forget that ordinary conflicts between children who spend all day together are completely expectable, that children grow a tougher skin from being with other children, that children also need to learn that grown-ups can occasionally be impatient and even mean. Sadly, of course, sometimes adults *are* cruel to children. And there are times when teachers act in overtly racist ways or display implicit bias that children can sense even if they cannot put it into words. Whatever the cause, when parents fear for their child's safety and well-being, they are likely to go on the attack.

Parent Fear 2: The teacher will judge my parenting negatively.

No parent is perfect. Even the best have trouble keeping up with their children's growth as they move from stage to stage. We'll explore this dilemma in more detail in the next two chapters. Here, we'll note that constantly trying to catch up to a child's developmental curve can leave one feeling like a rank amateur when, for example, a cheerful, compliant 5-year-old becomes a dawdling 6-year-old who resists all efforts to get dressed. Parents ask themselves, "What are we doing wrong?" Their self-doubts, large and small, can leave them feeling at risk of being exposed as incompetent in the teacher's eyes. They're not wrong.

At one time or another, all educators have indeed judged parents they don't know based on a child's behavior. An exasperated teacher who is having trouble with a student thinks, "If only this child had more sleep… if only this child didn't play so many video games… if only this child had been taught better manners…" and so on. It's easy to forgive a parent who forgets to pack a child's lunch once or twice. It's less easy when this becomes a pattern. No teacher wants to humiliate a parent, and most try not to be overtly critical. Most parents can acknowledge their occasional screwups. But there is no avoiding the potential for tension here.

In this regard, when parents have a concern, they may worry that the teacher will find the concern excessive or irrational. When talking with their child's adviser or the school counselor, many parents start a sentence with an apologetic, "I know this sounds crazy, but…." Having children can make parents feel that they are going out of their minds because they are trapped by their intense love for their children and their worries about them. There is no chart with a bright line that tells parents when they have crossed from rational to irrational. Every parent in the grip of such powerful feelings is capable of sounding overwrought, which can leave them confused and ashamed. Happily, in such situations most parents catch themselves and apologize for "losing it" even momentarily, or they warn a teacher or administrator about how strongly they feel in that moment about something affecting their child.

But some parents cannot always control themselves. Anyone who has watched a hard-fought athletic contest has seen parents behave badly—shouting at refs, at opposing players, at their own child; even complaining loudly about their child's coach. Understanding that parents sometimes reach an internal boiling point rapidly, even if they don't show it on the outside, is important for every educator.

Parent Fear 3: The teacher has huge power over my child.

This is a tough one for teachers to understand because they don't usually think of themselves as exercising a lot of power; they experience themselves as benevolent and trustworthy with children. But one wit observed that the most powerful person in the world is a kindergarten teacher on the first day of school. Teachers have power over children because they are the embodiment of natural authority. Alone and unobserved, they have students in class for whole days, weeks, and months. They express their power through their words, positive and negative; their rewards and punishments; and, of course, their grades.

There is a subtler power at work as well. It has long been known that the way a teacher views a student's academic potential can affect the teacher's interaction with that student and sometimes influence the student's performance. Even parents who don't know this research can wonder whether the teacher is really connecting with their child. That is why, when a child comes home and says, "The teacher doesn't like me," alarm bells go off for a parent.

When it comes to parents fearing teachers' power over children, the issues of assessment, grading, and placement are always going to be potential trouble spots between parents and schools. Parents naturally react strongly to having their child graded and assessed by a teacher because it raises the risk that a teacher could damage the child's future. Parents react angrily to a soccer coach's decision not to make their child a starter, to a drama teacher failing to give their child a lead part in the musical, and to a college adviser's list of possible colleges that don't match their expectations for their child. For some few parents, the last of these is *the* big disappointment at the end of a school career.

One final observation about parents' fears of teacher power involves the fear of retaliation. Many parents worry that if they complain about something the teacher or coach does, he or she will retaliate by taking it out on the child. In our experience, teachers hate to hear this and furiously deny that they would ever do it. And, indeed, we've almost never encountered actual examples of this occurring. But how could a parent not imagine it? We've even listened to faculty parents worry that a colleague, perhaps a drama teacher with whom they do not have a collegial relationship, will retaliate against them by denying their child a lead in the play.

How could a teacher-parent imagine such a thing? Actually, the fear of teacher retaliation isn't personal; it is simply universal.

Parent Fear 4: My most cherished dreams for my child may not come true.

All parents have dreams for their children when they send them off to school. Some dreams are spelled out in detail and are part of what we think of as the implicit psychological contract in the parents' minds when they mailed their tuition deposit ("I want her to be admitted to an elite college"). Other dreams are less definite ("I want her to reach her full potential" or "I want her to be happy"). But all dreams are at risk of colliding with real life. We have seen this many times with parents whose children are revealed to have a significant learning disability. The parental dream of having a gifted and happy student bangs up against that reality, and when a child is not thriving, parents are naturally concerned for the child but are also likely clinging to their original dream. Every learning specialist comes to expect the worries and occasional fury of parents.

Dreams are stubborn things. For many parents, the loss of a dream involves a process of grief, anger, and sometimes blame.

THREE FEARS OF TEACHERS

We have talked to literally thousands of teachers about the worries they carry into their relationship with parents. Like parents, teachers are afraid of being judged and found wanting, of being misunderstood, and, above all, of being in conflict with parents.

Teacher Fear 1: My mistakes will be on display in front of the distorting eyes of children.

This fear on the part of teachers is the mirror-image fear of parents who worry that the teacher will disapprove of their parenting. When a child comes home with a quirky or unhappy story about a teacher's behavior, especially one that sounds like the adult was intentionally mean or sarcastic to a child, it is highly likely that the parents will instantly judge the teacher. Teachers know that they are the subject of conversation in most households; it is not unreasonable of them to fear judgment. However, teachers sometimes forget that the vast majority of parents will check themselves, wonder about the context of the episode and aspects that the child may not have reported, and perhaps even consider their child's propensity for exaggeration or youthful lack of perspective.

A key contributor here is educators' sensitivity to disrespect. The cultural historian Jacques Barzun wrote that "teaching is not a lost art, but respect for it is a lost tradition."[2] Every educator feels society's disregard for teaching. It's expressed in, among other ways, significantly lower salaries than other professionals earn and denigrating humor ("Those who can, do; those who can't, teach"). Bringing out the best in children requires a combination of intelligence, training, and temperament, plus a special gift for taking young people seriously. But most adults simply do not understand how demanding it is to spend all day in a classroom with children, or how challenging it is to help struggling students learn. Teachers may wish that parents would be able to truly appreciate the complexities of their craft and their professionalism, but they don't expect it.

Most parental judgments of educators blow over; a new day, another story from a child, time moves on. But some judgments stick in a parent's mind and form the basis of an ongoing effort by the parent to ascertain the truth of what the child has said. We have seen lawyer parents try to follow up their child's anecdote by asking other parents, and sometimes other children, leading questions about the teacher. So teachers are not wrong to fear such parents. The problem is that teachers forget that these kinds of incidents are *extremely* rare, and most parents forget—or discount—their children's anecdotes. If teachers hold this fear too close to their heart, it makes them defensive and could possibly distort their work with both parents and their children.

Teacher Fear 2: I will see the student differently than parents do, and this may cause conflict.

Teachers tend to focus on the day-to-day struggles of the children in their class and the content of the curriculum they're teaching. In contrast, parents often have their eyes on the future, thinking about their child's long-term success and emotional well-being. For example, a teacher may worry that a third grade girl is not a good friend to her friends while her parent is focusing on the girl's self-confidence and leadership skills. Or in the case of an impulsive boy with a short attention span, the teacher may think, "How is this child going to be able to complete the assigned task? Is he ever going to be able to control himself through an entire class period?" At the same time, the parent may be thinking, "What do I do if the school recommends that he go on stimulant medication?"

As psychologists, we assume that people are going to start out with different assumptions and different goals; we expect that all of these will have to be, in the classic words of therapy, "worked through." Teachers often express the concern that conflicts with parents could arise in the course of their communications. They don't feel they have the training or the time to work through such conflicts. But for the most part they actually do so without even noticing, because the conflicts are normal and expectable. It is the possibility of larger conflicts, when huge gaps exist between parental hopes and the teacher's daily observations, that causes teachers to fear such conversations.

This brings us to perhaps teachers' biggest fear.

Teacher Fear 3: Administrators won't protect me from powerful parents.

One of the most common myths among faculties is that parents, especially wealthy or board member parents, are afforded special treatment and it is unsafe to upset them. We've seen this happen only a very few times. We have seen parents try to get teachers fired, but, in our experience, school administrators fight hard to protect their faculties from such interference.

Yet the fear of "heavy hitters" exists because there is, on average, a real disparity between the power and income of parents and those of teachers. A head of school in a wealthy Connecticut suburb once commented darkly, "I have come to understand the conflict between my parents and my teachers as class warfare." Indeed, teachers can easily see themselves as unprotected workers, even in a school where the head of school is a former teacher and believes—and says repeatedly—that great teaching is the heart of the school. We can say with conviction that we have never been in a school where teachers did *not* feel this vulnerability to a greater or lesser extent.

A major contributor to teachers' fear that they won't be protected is the growing frequency of irrational parent attacks. These events are not common, but they're not nearly as rare as they used to be. For many years we have been asking teachers how many of them are still carrying vivid memories of a verbal assault from a parent. Out of a faculty of a hundred, perhaps 25 or 30 teachers raise their hand, some reporting that even years later they are still capable of reliving the distress of it. Our worry is that such encounters, if not worked through and debriefed, could make a teacher wary and mistrustful of parents in general. One teacher, after describing a verbally assaultive and threatening father from years earlier, told us, "And now, whenever a parent comes into my room, I always think, 'Could this be one of those?'"

For most of us, good experiences are just assimilated into our psyches and bodies; bad experiences become encysted, and they hamper our functioning. Major outlier episodes of bad parent behavior affect not only the specific educator who is targeted but the faculty as a whole. News of the attack spreads rapidly. Teachers often overgeneralize from one case, and when they do, their attitudes toward parents can harden. And that's a shame, both for the teachers' career and for the parents coming down the road.

So a small number of teachers do harbor critical, angry, or condescending views of parents. This phenomenon is not widespread, but honesty compels us to report that it exists. There are teachers who hold parents in contempt, seeing them as overprivileged and indulgent of their children. Those who feel this way know that revealing these views can be risky, and so they try to minimize their contact with parents.

AN INHERENT IRONY

Any account of the normal tensions that underlie the parent-teacher relationship ends in irony. Parent and teacher are both deeply devoted to children, and each knows that the other is, too, but each is also potentially ready to fear and judge the other. Each wants what's best for the student, but their different roles and perspectives can cause them, at times, to disagree about precisely what *is* best.

As we have suggested, most of the time these issues are resolved quickly and amicably, which often strengthens the bond between educator and parent. But there are two additional sources of tension and sometimes conflict in the parent-teacher relationship. One is rooted in the psychosocial development of children. This is the subject of the next two chapters. We will address the second— accelerating change in the world and poor parenting advice—in Chapter 4.

ENDNOTES

[1] NAIS, *Why Do Parents Choose Independent Schools?* (Washington, DC), p. 2; online at https://www.nais.org/getmedia/959c0afd-3b41-46a0-b084-ec640e336685/Why-Do-Parents-Choose-Independent-Schools-JTBD-Booklet.pdf.

[2] Jacques Barzun, *Teacher in America* (Indianapolis, IN: The Liberty Fund, 1981), p. 15.

Factors rooted in children's psychosocial development are often sources of anxiety for parents—anxiety that they bring to their relationship with the school starting in the younger grades.

Chapter 2

Developmental Flashpoints: The Early Years

hildren make their parents crazy. That's a rule. They can drive their parents wild right from the start when, as babies, they develop colic or they don't sleep much or, later, because they are immature and impulsive or because they are needy and relentless. They're often deeply bewildering: When they're very young, they can't tell you what they want, and when they're older, they don't *want* to tell you what they're thinking. Parents spend much of their time one step behind the child's growth curve. They move in and out of confusion for the child's first 20 or so years. Most parents accept this state of affairs with more or less grace as part of the package of having a family. They don't generally burden the school with it.

Nonetheless, during the 14-year stretch from preschool to 12th grade, there are moments when the developmental growth of a child or the child's peers catches parents by surprise. They're blindsided by some unexpected behavior that previously seemed impossible. A seventh grade boy who's never been a problem at school is suspended for cheating and lying about it. His parents, shaken, come to school with a notebook listing every gold star, yellow smiley face, and complimentary note he has earned since kindergarten. He couldn't possibly be guilty of the alleged behavior, they argue, because he is such a *good* boy.

The problem here is not a sudden change in the boy's character; it's development. Many very good boys are suddenly not so law-abiding in seventh grade. This is rarely a surprise to a middle school teacher. It can be a real shock to parents.

We call moments like this "flashpoints." They almost always reflect the unfolding of developmental phases in the child and involve behaviors that are, for the most part, familiar and even predictable to educators. But often flashpoints are a sharp jolt for parents, who may respond with distressed and angry texts, emails, and calls to the school. Flashpoints are rooted in key areas of concern to every parent. We summarize these areas as separation, competition, social trauma, sex, and prejudice. Each is worth volumes in its own right. But in the interest of brevity, we offer an overview of factors rooted in children's psychosocial development that are often sources of anxiety for parents—anxiety that they bring to their relationship with the school. We begin in this chapter with the younger grades and turn to middle and upper school in the next chapter.

ELEMENTARY SCHOOL FLASHPOINTS

Separation

To be a parent is to be ambivalent. We "have" children, but we have to let them go. We want them to flourish at school and later in the wider world, but we worry each time they take another big or sudden step in that direction. The arc of development moves from dependence to independence, and as it does, major transitions are often flashpoints for parents.

As we've noted, the start of preschool and then kindergarten are emotional times for many, especially mothers. The bond of love between infant and mother, between small children and their parents, is one of the most powerful in human life. Loosening that bond can be a big adjustment. When parents are exceptionally anxious about leaving young children at school, they can make it hard for the children to undertake the transition. Helping both parents and children through the separation, calming parents' anxieties about leaving their children, is typically one of the gifts preschool and kindergarten teachers possess.

Competition

Parents worry that their child won't measure up. They're afraid that because of factors in the classroom or a developmental delay or deficit of some kind, a child will be at a competitive disadvantage, not just at the moment but perhaps throughout life. Some children learn to read by 3, others not until they're almost 7. Some don't complete toilet training until well after their peers. When parents fear that their child is lagging developmentally, they may panic or feel ashamed. This can happen as early as preschool and remain latent in parents throughout their children's school career.

Many independent school parents are also eager for their children to be "advanced." When their child is very young, they delight in the child's play and capacity to learn through experimentation, but they are also keen to have the child read and write and count early. When the child goes to kindergarten, they worry about academic progress. Some start to yearn for traditional markers of rigor. If the school and the teacher believe in the value of learning through play, parents can chafe about what they see as a need for more directed learning. Across the U.S., this is a tension in kindergartens in public and independent schools alike.

As students move through the early grades, it becomes clear that not all differences are due to immaturity. Some students do have delays or deficits in their academic, motor, or social capacities. Dyslexia, dysgraphia, gross and fine motor coordination, speech, and other developmental issues can be profoundly upsetting for parents. Teachers may refer children to learning specialists and occupational therapists. This can come as a shock to parents, even those who themselves have had some concerns about their child, when they feel they have been taken by surprise.

Social trauma

We humans are a highly—intensely—social species. We spend most of our lives preoccupied with status, with social comparisons. Even a casual observer can see that there is a complicated society in kindergarten, where some children are charismatic stars surrounded by a group and other children stay in quiet pairs. Many parents fear that their child may not develop friendships and will be excluded and lonely. And indeed, many kindergarten students come home with stories of exclusion and hurt feelings. Hearing too many such reports can persuade a parent that the teacher is not protecting the child.

Even in the early grades, students notice differences and make comparisons with one another. By second grade they are becoming what one head of school calls "super-sorters." Many boys, for example, can rank-order the others in athletic ability. By third and fourth grade, the compare-and-contrast tendency can sometimes harden into the scapegoating of a particular child. An impulsive and sometimes aggressive boy may no longer be invited on playdates or to birthday parties.

In this regard, parents cannot dictate whom their children befriend. Children make their own connections and naturally form groups, and they don't want to include kids they don't particularly like. Who's "in" and who's "out" can become a central dynamic, especially for girls. As they move into the later elementary years, a "mean girls" clique can form. Students who are charismatic or verbally assertive or top athletes may be able to throw their weight around, and their social and organizational power can morph into bullying. There is a built-in, irreducible minimum of conflict, tension, and social cruelty among children, just as among adults. Far too often, normal friction among students is incorrectly seen by parents as bullying, but when true bullying occurs, it can be devastating. Throughout their child's school journey, parents remain attentive to their child's social status and happiness. They can react sharply when the child complains of ill treatment or exclusion by peers, especially if this involves apparent bullying.

Sex and exploration

Of all the sources of developmental flashpoints, sex may be the most powerful. Parental concerns about their children's sexuality—and, more broadly, about the whole range of potentially risky exploratory behavior in which children engage— are more pronounced during middle and upper school. But the concerns start earlier. The very first girls to embark on pubertal development do so as early as fourth grade. Their bodies start to grow and change; they may display some breast development; and a very few may even start their periods by age 10. Because children are tuned into each other's bodies, these biological events introduce a note of social and hormonal tension in the class, which some parents may track and discuss. By fifth and sixth grade, the first hints of "gender intensification" are seen. Girls are needing to be beautiful or fashionable, and boys are needing to project that they are strong.

In our travels to schools, we hear many anecdotes about fifth and sixth graders who have been introduced to advanced internet content, R-rated movies, and pornography. A bold fifth grade boy who is a sophisticated consumer of the internet might bring his iPad to a sleepover to dazzle his friends by showing them porn sites. A rather more innocent boy, shocked by what he has seen, may confess to his parents what he saw and where, and they are likely to call the school to demand that it take action against the perpetrator. Leaving pornography aside, screen time itself—especially as it involves gaming and social media, not online learning—has become a common flashpoint in the elementary years and continues to be throughout the upper grades. Some parents are highly restrictive of their children's access to devices, others less so. The former often wish that the school would support them by setting a strict policy about this.

Prejudice

For parents of students of color, students from nondominant religions, and students from LGBTQ families, a potential flashpoint is prejudice. With reason, they are attentive to the ways in which their children might be subject to discrimination and bigotry. A racially tinged situation among students at any age may well cause parents to believe that their child is being subjected to systemic racism. Children tease one another, sometimes hurtfully. Teasing about clothing, religious beliefs, athletic acumen, poverty, or national origins can easily lead parents to conclude that widespread institutional bias exists against their child or their kind of family. The concerns in this area begin early. Children are observant. As early as preschool, they notice differences in skin color, clothes, hair, and weight, and they just flatly say what they see, such as "He's fat." They also come to blunt conclusions about the way society works and differences between families. A young student might say, "It's better to be white than Black," or "It's better to have a mom and dad than two moms."

When the student on the receiving end of any kind of prejudiced comments and behavior reports the event at home, it's likely that the school will get a call. Most schools proclaim a commitment to diversity, equity, and inclusion, but most, in our experience, struggle to implement this vow. Among the dilemmas schools encounter is that they feel caught between two sets of parents: those who want the school to fulfill its promise by educating children about racial and other differences, and those who protest that they're not ready to have their young children discuss race, adoption, or same-sex marriage.

In schools, just as in other spheres, "culture war" issues are potential flashpoints. As they move through the elementary years, children of color may begin to gather in their own groups in a more deliberate way. This is, in part, a reflection of a natural developmental tendency to connect to others with whom one shares important things in common. But it often makes teachers, especially white teachers, uncomfortable because it can potentially lead to charges and counter-charges of exclusion. Teachers should anticipate that parents may read this spontaneous grouping in this way, and they need to be prepared to speak directly with parents about race. We will explore this further in Chapter 6.

As children head off to middle school and then upper school, virtually all of the flashpoints mentioned in this chapter will recur, often in larger ways, and will be accompanied by new ones.

In adolescence, children yearn for space and privacy. Parents worry. And teachers and administrators land in the middle.

Chapter 3

Developmental Flashpoints: The Middle and Upper School Years

O nce when we were leading a workshop for parents at a K-12 school, we asked them to describe the ideal teacher.

"I wish my son's teacher would call me at the end of every school day and tell me what his day was like," one mother said.

We asked what grade her son was in.

"Tenth," she replied.

The audience laughed sympathetically while shaking their heads.

That's not going to happen in 10th grade, for lots of reasons. Middle school and upper school children are always seeking autonomy, separation, and individuation. They don't report everything to their parents, and they don't want the school to track them too closely either. For that reason, many of the developmental issues of adolescence come as a shock to parents. And it's why one of the most common parental complaints to a school about, say, a bad grade on a report card is "Why wasn't I warned about this?"

Throughout a child's school years, the five areas of parental worry discussed in the previous chapter are much the same: separation, competitive disadvantage, social trauma, identity, and sex—with additional elements of risk-taking (drugs and social media) now also a concern. But in adolescence these issues play out in the lives of children who are yearning for more space and privacy from their parents. Teachers and administrators can land in the middle. We often hear from high school advisers that just as a student starts to open up, he or she will suddenly pause and ask, "You won't tell my parents, will you?"

HOW THE FIVE AREAS OF WORRY PLAY OUT IN ADOLESCENCE

Separation

For parents, the painful aspects of separation in the middle school years are psychological rather than physical. By about age 11, most children are starting to push back on their parents' authority. This manifests itself as stubbornness, disobedience, not wanting to join parents in a social gathering, and—above all—a wish for privacy, particularly with respect to their social lives.

This loss of closeness and control hits parents hard. Teachers in middle school often find that parents are trying to get information from them that they cannot get directly from their own children. Sometimes parents press teachers to give their children the very advice the children are ignoring at home. Teachers may find it hard to say no to a pushy parent even when they know that the intervention is going to fail.

As eighth graders head to high school, parents often imagine that the transition is a scary prospect for their child. Not in our experience! Most eighth graders are eager to leave the restrictions of middle school, and some ambitious eighth grade girls already have their sights set on older boys. As sophomores and juniors grow more independent, parents complain that they "never see them." Many moms and dads are thrilled by the college admissions process because they feel licensed to supervise this last chapter for their child—arranging college visits, helping edit the personal essay, and so on. This often creates conflicts that college counselors find themselves managing. The intensity of the college process is, at the deepest level, driven by a parent's anticipation of impending separation: the end of childhood.

Competitive disadvantage

As children enter the academic grades that "really count," parental vigilance leads mothers and fathers to grow more sensitive to any indication that a child may be at a disadvantage.

Many sixth graders develop an interest that may bloom into a passion—one that then becomes very important to parents and their vision of the student's future. Some students, however, don't focus on one sport or activity. They are not fully engaged, and parents worry that teachers may be giving their child short shrift. If the student isn't placed in an honors math class, or doesn't get a leading part in the play, or doesn't become a starter on the soccer team, parents can imagine that the child's entire future will be affected. Not all students belong in honors math, and not all aspiring actors can handle the lead in a musical. But when a teacher or coach makes a decision that disappoints parents, there may well be a strong reaction.

Social trauma

The middle school years are, without question, the toughest socially for most children. Early adolescents are hormonally drawn to one another and wired to be exquisitely attuned to social cues. What is happening with their friends matters more than *anything*. Because they love their friends and feel so strongly about acceptance, middle school students can be manipulated by others. Girl cliques, which have been forming since fourth grade, ramp up in sixth grade and peak in seventh. The "mean girls" who are at the top of the popularity ladder have the power to exclude—and they use it. The early-developing boys with bigger muscles and deeper voices can start to dominate in seventh and eighth grade, throwing their weight around—literally!

Parents of smaller boys or less popular girls stand by helplessly, feeling for their children and trying to understand the difference between the normal jockeying for social position and actual bullying. Children report that parents are always checking on their social lives, sometimes daily. As a sixth grade boy said, "My mother is always asking me about my friends. She must think I'm a loser." By eighth grade, most children have convinced their parents to stop asking, either by repeated rebuffs or by displays of social competence.

Because experiments in the uses and abuses of social power are a temptation to middle school children, it is the responsibility of teachers to make their classes as safe and civil as they possibly can. However, for some parents, especially those with unresolved feelings from their own middle school years, the classroom can never be safe enough. When parents see ordinary social conflict between children as bullying and the school does not, that can be a big flashpoint.

Identity

Adolescence is a time of identity formation. Teenage conversations turn on questions of "Who am I?" "Who are we?" "Who are they?" As students in middle and early high school become abstract thinkers, they start to tackle larger social issues that haunt adult society, including racism. The conversations aren't always nice; they can lead to conflict. The memorable title of Beverly Tatum's book *Why Are All the Black Kids Sitting Together in the Cafeteria?*[1] captured the confusion that some educators and parents experience as many children of color apparently self-segregate as a component of racial identity development. What many high school students of color experience from the majority of their white classmates is cluelessness or casual racism. When asked why he had chosen to attend a historically Black college, the first student from his independent school to do so, one graduating Black senior replied, "I am tired of educating white people."

While the majority of students identify as cis-gender and heterosexual, trans and nonbinary students and gay, lesbian, and bisexual students also make their own journeys. If a gay or trans student is going to come out publicly at school, it is likely to be during the middle or high school years. Who accepts this, who doesn't, and how the school responds (about bathrooms, participation in sports teams, and so on) are the flashpoints that can divide the parent body.

In this regard, there are parents who believe that a school should be an oasis from conversations about tough social issues such as racism or homophobia. They are shocked by how raw the debates can be at the middle and high school level, and they sometimes hold the school responsible for letting things get out of control.

Sex, drugs, and risk-taking

Of all the sources of developmental flashpoints, sex may be the most common. Here again, as everywhere in parenting, there is ambivalence. No parents want their son or daughter to be left out of the adolescent social world, which obviously includes physical attraction and romantic feelings. But all parents find it easy to worry that their child may experiment too early and too much with sex.

We know a middle school principal who tells parents on back-to-school night, "When you send your children to us, they are *babies*; when they leave us, they can *have* babies." Seventh and eighth graders live in a hormonal storm. Everyone is keenly aware of their developmental status. Children are physically attracted to one another. Some try early, tentative sexual activity. *Everyone* is thinking about sex. By the time they leave 10th grade, 20% of students are not just thinking about sex; they've had sex. By the time they graduate, the percentages rise to 53% for girls and to 48% for boys.[2] A worrisome 40% of sexually active teenage girls have contracted a sexually transmitted disease.[3]

Sex is, of course, just one of the areas in which adolescents experiment and parents worry. Juniors and seniors tend to be the biggest risk-takers in school. They have driver's licenses; many have begun to smoke marijuana and drink; and parties, too often marked by binge drinking, are the high point of many of their weekends. Almost 70% of high school seniors will have tried alcohol, and more than half, an illegal drug. The latter can be part of a pattern of risky behavior that includes both unsafe sex and driving while intoxicated.[4]

Parents' concerns about their children's exploration extend beyond sex and substances to screen time and social media. These are venues where children find access to the entire content of the adult world, including all sorts of material that is unfiltered by their parents and teachers.

Families and schools continue to grapple with how best to integrate use of screens for learning, entertainment, and social interaction. A minority of parents greatly restrict their children's access to TV and technology. Others are more accommodating but continue to be anxious about the risks. At literally every parent talk we give, there are questions about screen time and digital devices. Parents fret about the risk that children will become addicted to their devices (devices the parents bought for them), about predators online, and about

R-rated movies and pornography—all of which represent for them their children's loss of innocence. Children arrive at this loss at different ages depending on whether they have older siblings and how closely their parents supervise them, among other things. In this regard, children are readily exposed to pornography. Although detailed statistics are difficult to collect, it appears that at least 30% of boys and almost 25% of girls have viewed some pornography by the age of 13.[5]

Abundant anecdotal evidence suggests that parents underestimate the extent and content of their children's online activity. But every school knows that parents are likely to react intensely to episodes of sexual interest and behavior (sexting, for example).

There is one more source of parental anxiety related to the vulnerability and impulsivity of adolescence that can spark a flashpoint: suicide. It would be wrong to say that parents routinely worry about their child potentially taking his or her own life, but a child's suicide is every parent's worst nightmare. Self-inflicted death is rare among school-age children. Although there has been an increase in the rate among this age group, it remains vastly lower than among adults.[6] Nonetheless, there is something especially tragic about young people who kill themselves. When it does occur, it is likely to ignite a firestorm of concern among students, parents, and faculty. In their grief and helplessness, parents are more likely than in the past to blame the death on school pressure and stress, even though research into suicide points strongly to mental illness and family factors, not school influences.[7]

BEYOND SCHOOL

The underlying worries that can trigger flashpoints are embedded in child development and parenting. At a deep level, these worries have always been there, built into human nature. It's impossible to imagine a flashpoint-free school, one in which no parent is reactive to the kinds of issues outlined here.

But only in the past few decades have schools been pressured—and have they also, on their own, volunteered—to attempt to prevent many of the flashpoints. The effort is both noble and understandable; it is, after all, what the customers want. But the attempt is a struggle, in part because the flashpoints occur at school but are not *caused* by the school. Nor are they within the school's power and reach in the way that many parents and educators hope. As we shall see, this is to a large degree because of larger social changes and a pronounced and unhelpful shift in the advice parents consume.

ENDNOTES

[1] Beverly Daniel Tatum, *Why Are All the Black Kids Sitting Together in the Cafeteria? And Other Conversations About Race* (New York: Basic Books, 1997).

[2] Joyce C. Abma and Gladys M. Martinez, "Sexual Activity and Contraceptive Use Among Teenagers in the United States: 2011-2015," *National Health Statistics Reports*, June 22, 2017; online at https://www.cdc.gov/nchs/data/nhsr/nhsr104.pdf. Jochen Peter and Patti M. Valkenburg, "Adolescents and Pornography: A Review of 20 Years of Research," *Journal of Sex Research*, Special Issue, "Annual Review of Sex Research," 53, nos. 4-5 (2016); online at https://www.tandfonline.com/doi/full/10.1080/00224499.2016.1143441.

[3] Sara E. Forhan et al., "Prevalence of Sexually Transmitted Infections Among Female Adolescents Aged 14 to 19 in the United States," *Pediatrics*, December 2009, pp. 1505-1512; online at https://pediatrics.aappublications.org/content/124/6/1505.long.

[4] National Institute on Drug Abuse, *Principles of Adolescent Substance Use Disorder Treatment: A Research-Based Guide* (Washington, DC: 2014); online at https://www.drugabuse.gov/publications/principles-adolescent-substance-use-disorder-treatment-research-based-guide/introduction.

[5] Chiara Sabina, Janis Wolak, and David Finkelhor, "The Nature and Dynamics of Internet Pornography Exposure for Youth," *CyberPsychology & Behavior* 11, no. 6 (2008); online at http://www.unh.edu/ccrc/pdf/CV169.pdf.

[6] National Institute of Mental Health, Mental Health Information, "Suicide"; online at https://www.nimh.nih.gov/health/statistics/suicide.shtml.

[7] David A. Brent and Nadine Melhem, "Familial Transmission of Suicidal Behavior," *Psychiatric Clinics of North America* 31, no. 2 (2008): 157-177; online at https://www.ncbi.nlm.nih.gov/pmc/articles/PMC2440417/. American Academy of Pediatrics, "Teen Suicide, Mood Disorder, and Depression," July 2011; online at https://pediatrust.com/Teen-Suicide-Mood-Disorder-and-Depression. American Academy of Pediatrics, "Talking About 13 Reasons Why & Teen Suicide: Tips for Parents," October 18, 2016; online at https://www.healthychildren.org/English/health-issues/conditions/emotional-problems/Pages/Teen-Suicide-Statistics.aspx.

As if the loss of predictability in the world weren't anxiety-producing enough, parents are besieged by simplistic "strategies" to prevent danger and promote success.

Chapter 4

Big Changes, Bad Advice

Parents' predispositions to be anxious about dealing with their children's teachers and about developmental flashpoints are both normal. Nevertheless, they have been greatly magnified by two key factors, among others: rapid social and economic change and an epidemic of counterproductive childrearing advice. Taken together, these factors have undermined parents' confidence and complicated their approach to school.

ONE BIG CHANGE: THE LOSS OF PREDICTABILITY

One way to understand the larger causes of parental anxiety is to start from the opposite end and ask what conditions would be essential to helping parents feel confident about their childrearing. For us, two conditions immediately stand out: The rate of change would need to be slow and the choices for children, few.

Imagine a primitive Stone Age fishing village in which the men fish and the women dry fish. The pace of change is glacial, the options for children are nonexistent, and the certainty for parents is sky-high. A son must learn to fish, a daughter, to dry fish. Roles are clear and fixed. Everyone is certain about what the future will require: exactly what the present requires.

Simplistic? Of course, although it's actually not that far from how most people have lived for most of human history. The point here is that in 21st century America, we imagine, falsely, that the context in which we raise children is normal. But by any historical measure, it is way out on the far reaches of human experience. Our world is changing ever faster—almost none of what is happening today was predictable even five years ago. And virtually all children are now supposed to be able to become anything they want, live anywhere they want, and live any way they want. The unprecedented freedom and opportunity are fabulous. But the certainty for parents is low. Roles are less clear, more fluid. No one can predict what the future will require—except that it will likely be very different from what the present requires.

This loss of predictability started long ago, but it began accelerating in the 1960s and has soared since 2000. America has moved from a fairly stable, standardized life cycle based on long-term employment in the industrial economy to a destabilized, destandardized life cycle based on much less permanent employment in our current information/entrepreneurial economy. By the 1950s, work life had come to be organized along four principles that made people's lives more certain: steady work, mutual loyalty, rising pay, and what in retrospect looks like limited effort. There was an assumption of mutual loyalty and shared goals between employee and employer—no company that was profitable laid people off. Compensation was based on seniority more than output (as indeed it still is in most schools), and so people could rely on their salaries to rise over time.[1]

What has happened since the 1960s is by now a well-known story. The new economy began to destroy and restructure, with astonishing rapidity, the entire edifice of American life. Electronic communication, social media, deregulation, and globalization shattered the longstanding security of corporate oligopolies. A dynamic renewal of American entrepreneurship began transforming America's companies from fat and happy to lean and mean. This has generated exceptional growth and innovation, which have resulted in a constantly expanding array of products, services, and investments. The internet, social media, and communications technology have intensified competition among sellers of products and shortened the shelf life of innovations. This in turn begets even more innovation and productivity because, to survive, organizations must keep cutting their costs, adding value to their existing products and services, and creating new ones.

As has been widely reported—and rued—this brave new world has sharply raised the living standards of professional families, but it has also caused enormous economic and social dislocation. Its impact on the parts of life that depend on relationships, continuity, and stability—marriage, family, schooling, religion—has been problematic. As former Secretary of Labor Robert Reich has noted, "The faster the economy *changes* the harder it is for people to be confident of *what any of us will earn* next year or even next month, what they will be doing, where they will be doing it."[2] Predictability is vanishing. Work is no longer steady, and compensation doesn't rise systematically, especially for those who rely on the gig economy and are hired by the hour or the project, without benefits. Employers' loyalty has withered; profitable corporations earning billions don't hesitate to shed staff to further improve the bottom line.

Much of the controversy about the new economy has focused on the way it has vaporized factory jobs and upended the lives of those who perform routine work; widened the income gap between the skilled and the unskilled; and hollowed out retail stores, downtowns, shopping malls, and so on. But large numbers of independent school parents are white-collar professionals, and however concerned they might have been about the consequences of the new economy, most didn't have to worry that these threatened their own children—at first. Now entrepreneurial and technological change has been relentlessly climbing the white-collar ladder, leaving parents—including those who are doing well at the moment—increasingly uncertain about how to guarantee a secure future for their children.

For example, not long ago, parents could have every confidence that medicine and law would be ideal destinations for their sons and daughters. No longer. Consider:

- For years now, doctors, as a group, have been reporting declining job satisfaction and higher stress and burnout. Their work lives have been consumed by red tape, pressures to speed appointments and maximize billable visits, and the burdens of electronic recordkeeping. All this is a poor reward for medical school tuition that, in 2020, averaged between $150,000 and $250,000 and has left many with massive debt.[3] The suicide rate among physicians is the highest of any profession and more than twice that of the general population.[4]

- Until the 1990s, a law degree was an affordable conduit to a predictable, well-paid future. But law school tuitions have quadrupled over the past 25 years, and new lawyers now graduate with an average debt exceeding $120,000. Meanwhile, online legal services have been devouring entry-level jobs and disrupting the profession's longstanding stability and security. Top firms still offer handsome starting salaries and lucrative careers, but in the field more broadly, employment and incomes are much, much softer than they used to be. Seventy-five percent of lawyers surveyed by the Gallup Poll say that their law degree was not worth the cost.[5]

- Technology is now threatening other white-collar careers. It appears that the burgeoning field of artificial intelligence will disproportionately displace well-compensated professionals like market research analysts, sales managers, computer programmers, personal financial advisers, and management analysts.[6]

- Thanks to the loss of stable, benefit-paying jobs and to stagnant wages, mounting student loan debt, and rising rents, among other factors, a record proportion of young adults—22% of 24- to 34-year-olds—were living at home with their parents in 2019. This compares to 10% of people in the same age group in 2000.[7]

Of all the anxiety sparked by uncertainty about the future, the most visible to educators may be worry about "admission up." Parents' focus on college admission has long been on the rise, feeding—and fed by—a cottage industry of private admissions counselors and test prep companies. Even though schools' own college counselors have always known that there are at least several hundred (if not thousand) postsecondary institutions where students can receive an excellent education, the loss of predictability has inclined ever more parents to concentrate on a small number of well-known colleges. This frenzy—as many schools' counselors describe it—helped make possible the stunning, infamous "Varsity Blues" cheating scandal, discovered in 2019, in which wealthy parents were found to have paid huge sums to get their children admitted illegally to some of these colleges.[8]

But the admission anxiety, once mostly confined to college, has been creeping downward. Elementary and middle schools must now manage pressure from parents of students who are in their final year. As one school head told us:

> Many more parents now say some version of "If she doesn't get admitted to X school next year, this will have been a waste"—not "This was wonderful and we want her to get admitted to X." It's like we're just the vehicle to get her into X.

Any school would resent being seen only as a conduit, but viewed strictly from the perspective of a parent who is scared about the future, the admission up anxiety is understandable.

ANOTHER PROBLEM: BAD ADVICE

As if the loss of predictability weren't anxiety-provoking enough for parents, they've been further besieged by an onslaught of poor childrearing advice.

There are now several thousand books on parenting, most presenting ways to prevent problems in children and to accelerate their development and academic achievement. In the service of helping parents be more confident and successful, this pop literature, taken as a whole, instead offers recurring reasons for parents to doubt and second-guess themselves. There is a terrible irony here. The scientific knowledge base about children's psychosocial development has grown hugely since the 1960s, and the central core of what's been learned should lift parents' confidence because it confirms that most children are capable copers. Instead, a swelling chorus of writers to whom parents turn present children as fundamentally fragile and potentially at risk. These writers also press upon parents a range of dubious, simplistic, and contradictory "strategies" to prevent danger and promote success.

The advances in understanding child development have been vast. Much more is known than ever before about the interplay of nature and nurture; about the impact on development of biology, genes, and heredity; and about familial, social, cultural, and economic influences. A key theme in this large body of research is that *most children are mostly resilient*. All children have fragile moments, and some truly are fragile. But the research shows overwhelmingly that most are not. The majority of children turn out to be resilient and adaptive—even in the face of significant challenges—provided that they grow up with at least basic amounts of predictable care and nurture; with relatively clear structures to guide behavior; and with adequate freedom to learn from the consequences of their experience and to master developmentally appropriate challenges.

Most of the advice industry, however well-meaning, ignores or misrepresents this fundamental finding. Many books either don't draw on the knowledge base at all or do so only selectively, exaggerating both children's potential vulnerabilities and the ways parents can avoid them. Since the 1990s, for example, pop literature has concentrated heavily first on self-esteem and then on trauma—subjecting both words to significant definition creep.

Self-esteem has become one of the most widely known child development concepts. Technically, it refers to one's subjective evaluation of one's own worth. There is no question that it feels better to have a positive, rather than a negative, sense of oneself, or that it benefits children to see themselves as capable copers. However, readers of the advice literature have been told for decades that self-esteem can be promoted by positive reinforcement, which, in turn, promotes performance in academics and other spheres. This view has permeated American education, especially in lower schools, where many teachers routinely compliment even students' most modest achievements.

Unfortunately, this view of self-esteem is false.

The research has long been clear that elaborate praise and trophies for all do not build a strong inner core in a child or foster future success academically, athletically, or socially. On the contrary, what strengthens children's self-confidence is tackling and eventually mastering developmentally appropriate challenges. Academic success contributes to self-esteem, not the reverse.[9] One can read extensively in the advice literature and encounter this truth only rarely.

Trauma, like self-esteem, has also been exaggerated and misapplied by many advice writers. They portray all sorts of common events as potentially traumatic. True psychological trauma is an emotional response to an extreme, shocking event such as a terrible accident, physical or sexual abuse, or a natural disaster. There is persuasive evidence that what have come to be called adverse childhood experiences (ACEs), when they occur in combination with one another, can, in severe cases, exert a trauma-like impact on children. These experiences range from economic insecurity and parental divorce through physical and sexual abuse and growing up in a dysfunctional family. Children who grow up in poverty and in truly dysfunctional families are much more likely than others to suffer ACEs. Far too many children endure these conditions.

But the vast majority of the difficulties, disappointments, frustrations, and upsets encountered by the vast majority of children—especially those whose families can afford independent school tuition—are not disabling traumas.

Another flaw in the literature is that much of it sees childrearing as the application of expertise.

Parenting was once understood largely as a matter of natural competence rooted in intuition and experience, and developmentally savvy writers used to emphasize how children progress through a natural sequence of stages.

Now many writers present parenting as a matter of deliberate techniques (often fancified as "strategies")—a change described by the eminent psychologist David Elkind as moving from "how do" to "how to" (how does child's development naturally unfold vs. how can you accelerate your child's development). Much of the emphasis today is on methods to achieve specific outcomes, often through a one-size-fits-all approach, as though the same technique would be suited to children of any age or disposition.[10] All parents need some techniques to raise their children—none could survive a week without some sort of maneuver—and many advice books include some sensible tactics. But the idea that childrearing can be *based on* tactics and *built upon* professional expertise ends up disabling rather than empowering parents. It increases their anxiety instead of reducing it, leaves them vulnerable to whiplash as they read different books, and stimulates them to be ever more perfectionistic and vigilant in avoiding problems.

Ignoring the truth that most children are mostly resilient, the books foster what psychologist Robert White called an "overdriven striving," an intense desire for supposedly healthy traits that makes parents worry "at even a hint of the opposite traits."[11]

In this regard, to travel widely in schools is to hear frequent faculty complaints about today's younger parents, even from today's younger teachers. Educators we talk to everywhere worry about several trends: Parents see parenting too much as a performance, with their children as a kind of product. Parents are highly competitive about their child's accomplishments compared to those of their classmates. Parents try too hard to accelerate early academic and cognitive development. Parents expose young children to too much technology, despite evidence that this can compromise cognitive and social development.

And parents are excessively preoccupied with safety—they worry too much about children's risk-taking, even though free play, which can sometimes be risky, is one of the best ways children develop confidence, resilience, and problem-solving skills.

Although these trends may be more pronounced among younger parents, they have been spreading and intensifying for years and now form the dominant narrative about parents in most of the schools we visit.

PREPARING THE PATH FOR THE CHILD

It is important to reiterate here what we said at the outset of this book: The large majority of independent school parents are good people who send to the school good kids and who, at heart, want to be good participants in the school community.

But major social and economic changes have, understandably, raised their anxiety, which advice writers, hoping to be helpful but ignoring or mistranslating the key findings about psychosocial development, have further fueled. The combination has fostered a vigilant perfectionism, a sense that everything must go right or a child's future could suffer permanent blight. It inclines parents to approach the school predisposed to be anxious, demanding consumers.

At commencement ceremonies, many school heads like to speak of education as a journey. But for reasons not fully in parents' control, it seems that today large numbers of parents want the school to help them prepare the path for their child instead of preparing their child for the path.

ENDNOTES

[1] Jerald Wallulis, *The New Insecurity: The End of the Standard Job and Family* (Albany: State University of New York Press, 1998), pp. 2-3. Robert B. Reich, *The Future of Success: Working and Living in the New Economy* (New York: Knopf, 2001), pp. 5-6, 93-94, 17. Robert H. Frank, *Luxury Fever: Weighing the Cost of Excess* (New York: Free Press, 1999), p. 33.

[2] Reich, *Future of Success*, p. 7 (emphasis in original), pp. 98-103, 83-85.

[3] Rebecca Lake, reviewed by Marguerita Cheng, "Average Cost of Medical School," *The Balance*, September 25, 2020; online at https://www.thebalance.com/average-cost-of-medical-school-4588236.

[4] Pauline Anderson, "Physicians Experience Highest Suicide Rate of Any Profession," *Medscape*, May 7, 2018; online at https://www.medscape.com/viewarticle/896257.

[5] Zac Auter, "Few MBA, Law Grads Say Their Degree Prepared Them Well," Gallup, February 16, 2018; online at https://news.gallup.com/poll/227039/few-mba-law-grads-say-degree-prepared.aspx?g_source=link_NEWSV9&g_medium=NEWSFEED&g_campaign=item_&g_content=Few%20MBA,%20Law%20Grads%20Say%20Their%20Degree%20Prepared%20Them%20Well.

[6] Mark Muro, Jacob Whiton, and Robert Maxim, *What Jobs Are Affected by AI?* (Washington, DC: Brookings Institution, 2019), p. 5; online at https://www.brookings.edu/wp-content/uploads/2019/11/2019.11.20_BrookingsMetro_What-jobs-are-affected-by-AI_Report_Muro-Whiton-Maxim.pdf#page=5.

[7] Jamie Anderson, "Mothers & Their Millennials: Where Working-Age Millennials Are Still Living with Mom," Zillow, May 4, 2016; online at https://www.zillow.com/research/millennials-living-with-mom-12287/. Richard Fry, "It's Becoming Common for Young Adults to Live at Home—and for Longer Stretches," Pew Research Center, Fact Tank, May 5, 2017; online at https://www.pewresearch.org/fact-tank/2017/05/05/its-becoming-more-common-for-young-adults-to-live-at-home-and-for-longer-stretches/.

[8] Axios, "Timeline: The Major Developments in the College Admissions Scandal," August 21, 2020; online at https://www.axios.com/college-admission-scandal-operation-varsity-blue3s-51e66764-23b2-4539-ba05-d55740939c46.html.

[9] Roy F. Baumeister, Jennifer D. Campbell, Joachim I. Krueger, and Kathleen D. Vohs, "Exploding the Self-Esteem Myth," *Scientific American Mind*, December 2005, pp. 50-57.

[10] David Elkind, *All Grown Up and No Place to Go* (Reading, MA: Addison-Wesley, 1998), pp. 11-12, 14, 248.

[11] Robert White, *Lives in Progress: A Study of the Natural Growth of Personality* (New York: Holt, Rinehart, and Winston, 1966), p. 407.

PART 2

CHALLENGES

It's important to understand why some parents act the way they do and why the ways in which schools have traditionally dealt with them can be ineffective.

■

There's a fundamental distinction between the vast majority of parents—the "95 percenters" who can be worked with—and a small minority—the "5 percenters" who can disrupt the school community.

Chapter 5

Parents: A Behavioral Typology

When educators refer to "the parents"—particularly when voicing a concern or complaint about them—they generally speak as though parents were a monolithic block. They're not. In our experience, they divide broadly into two groups, which we think of, in shorthand, as "95 percenters" and "5 percenters." This division doesn't derive from formal research or statistical analysis. It reflects our decades of experience helping schools manage their relationships with parents. We could have written "the vast majority and the small minority" or "the mostly reasonable and the mostly unreasonable." We use "95 percenters" and "5 percenters" because teachers and administrators have told us that they find this characterization intuitively accurate, easy to remember, and helpful.

THE 95 PERCENTERS

The parents we call 95 percenters are workable. We often summarize them to a faculty just as we have in this book, as "good people who send good students and who want to be positive participants in the school community." Teachers invariably agree, when we ask them, that this characterizes most of their parents.

To be sure, 95 percenters are not as workable as they were several decades ago, when the school's institutional authority was much stronger than it is today. These parents are subject to the rising tide of anxiety we've described. There are now many more of them for whom everything about school is fine—as long as everything is fine—and many more who become quickly distressed when a problem that involves their child—even a small issue—arises. They are, on average, less ready to simply accept a teacher's judgment about what's best for a student's learning and growth, especially if the student shows even a small sign of upset about this. They are more likely to take as literal truth what a child, even a very young one, says about an episode that happened in school. They are also notably more likely than parents were in the past to ask for exceptions to a teacher's discipline of their child or to the school's discipline policy.

Even with all of this and even when they are genuinely distressed, most parents can be helped and calmed and reasoned with. They may become very upset, something that happens to virtually every parent at some point during a child's schooling. But they can be comforted by being given some extra time— meeting with the teacher, being listened to, hearing a cogent explanation delivered with sweet reason. Teachers' knowledge of their craft, their generous hearts, their empathy, and their understanding of students all help them address the concerns of most parents and bring most situations to a satisfactory conclusion. This doesn't always happen quickly; there can be conflict and confusion. It may require several meetings and include administrators and possibly other specialists.

But in the end, the educators involved find common ground with the parent, and the matter gets resolved.

THE 5 PERCENTERS

The parents we call 5 percenters are different. Very. They cannot be soothed or reasoned with, no matter how hard the school tries. For a number of sad psychological reasons, they provoke and sustain an abrasive, aggrieved, unhappy, mistrustful relationship with the school, sometimes for years. In some cases, their criticism is relentless. In others, it's episodic; it emerges, seems to be resolved, but then reemerges—and keeps repeating this pattern. In the worst instances, these parents become widely feared and avoided by everyone at school, grow to be the focus of faculty room conversations, and cause teachers and coaches to whom their children are assigned to lose sleep. Ultimately, their complaints and behavior require administrative intervention.

Educators often find it very hard to understand why some parents cannot form and sustain a cooperative, trusting relationship with them. One immediate cause is mental illness. Schools assume that the families they admit are mentally healthy. Most are. However, roughly one-quarter of American adults suffer from a diagnosable mental disorder in any given year.[1] Anxiety and depression are the most common conditions, followed by substance abuse issues, phobias, and PTSD from past traumatic events. For the most part, people with these disorders continue to function effectively. Five percent of people have far more serious illnesses, including schizophrenia, psychoses, and character disorders.[2] There is not a perfect overlap between the most troubled 5% of the general population and the 5 percenters in independent schools. But it is not zero; every school community includes a small subset of people with serious mental health problems.

A second cause of difficulty in forming a cooperative relationship with a school stems from childhood trauma. Research suggests that at least 10% of the adults in the U.S. endured some sort of sexual abuse as children.[3] (The vulnerability is greater among children who grow up in poverty, so the incidence may be lower among independent school parents.) These experiences may have caused greater or lesser degrees of trauma, which in turn may have affected these parents' ability to trust others, especially authority figures. Most of them have found love, a trustworthy partner, and stability in their lives; perhaps through therapy, they have worked through their PTSD and mistrust.

But others have not. Consider how difficult it could be for a profoundly mistrustful survivor parent to send a child to school. It's not hard to see why such people might choose an independent school for their child, but they are likely to continue to worry that the child might not be adequately protected. A small and normal incident—say, two kindergarten children showing each other their genitals—could rekindle a parent's earlier trauma and cause an explosion.

Three Types of 5 Percenters

When a teacher or administrator is working with a 95 percenter, there may be tremors in the conversation, but the ground stays solid under their feet. With 5 percenters, there is no sure footing. They can overwhelm teachers because they are typically driven by their own demons more than by their child's actual situation. Five percenters include a range of parents, among them depressed and anxious people who suffer from clinical levels of mental illness; those with character disorders who distort reality in paranoid, narcissistic ways and make others suffer; those who are in terrible marriages or who are divorced and locked in endless, bitter custody battles; and truly entitled members of the upper class who feel that the bourgeois school rules do not apply to their children.

What 5 percenter parents have in common is that they are virtually immune to insight and therefore almost impossible to manage. They have virtually no capacity—or appetite—for self-reflection. They almost never ask themselves, "Am I doing something to upset people or that keeps them from seeing things my way?" Trying to reach them through extended rational discussion is fruitless. They fall into three primary types: anxious and incompetent; unresponsive; and intimidating.

- **Anxious and incompetent parents.** These types don't put teachers off; they pull them in, at least at first. By "anxious" here, we refer not to the general varieties of anxiety we've outlined in the preceding chapters but to a more serious, clinical condition. There are parents who suffer from a pervasive anxiety that they often can't control and that leaves them in chronic need of reassurance and support.

  For their part, educators are caregivers who are sensitive to distress in others and who want to be helpful. They almost always know how to empathize with upset students and then get them back on task. But educators find it much tougher to set limits with parents. In virtually every school we visit, we encounter several cases in which teachers are being inundated by texts, emails, and calls from a worried parent—communication that might have seemed, at first, potentially helpful in supporting the student's journey but that has turned into a burden. Almost invariably, the teachers, trapped by their own good hearts, have kept up the communication largely out of a sense that the parent needs it. We also hear frequently about clinically anxious parents who present as helpless and try to engage the teacher in matters that they themselves should undertake, such as telling students to stop fighting with their siblings, to stop playing with a certain friend, or even to eat their vegetables!

Accommodating a parent's anxiety disorder can quickly become a slippery slope: Each request the teacher accepts makes it harder to refuse the next.

- **Unresponsive parents.** The 5 percenters who are sometimes the most heartbreaking for educators are the ones who deny serious concerns that the school reports about a student and won't get the child the needed help. Some are disengaged from their child. Some are frightened by parenting and ashamed to admit it. Others have a family secret (substance abuse, a bad marriage, sexual abuse, criminal behavior) that they don't want to expose to the school. And still others, for reasons of narcissism, simply can't acknowledge that their child may have a "defect" and doesn't fit the standard profile of students at the school.

  Every school can cite a number of cases in which a student manifests serious early learning problems and the teacher asks for a screening by the learning specialist but the parents won't approve, or the parents arrange for testing by an outside evaluator but then refuse to share the results with the school. In either case, the school may then back off for a year, with the educators trying their best but also hoping that the shock of having a learning-disabled child will diminish and the parents will agree to full cooperation. But the denying and unresponsive parents never do.

- **Intimidating parents.** As difficult as it can be to calm the clinically anxious, encourage the incompetent, and get through to the unresponsive, the hardest 5 percenters to cope with are the intimidators. Some parents are so accustomed to wealth and power that they treat everyone, including educators, as though they were servants. They condescend, even without meaning to. They expect to be listened to and obeyed—to tell, not to be told.

Other intimidators, when they feel helpless or frightened about their child, react by attacking the teacher and the school. Their attacks are often personal: The parents don't just object to something a teacher is doing or not doing; they accuse the teacher of malpractice, not caring, pursuing a vendetta against their child, and so on.

Whatever the cause, intimidating parents are among the very toughest to handle because most teachers—and many administrators— are highly conflict-avoidant. They didn't choose a life in education because they love to mix it up with other adults. They try to explain and justify their actions, decisions, and recommendations about a student, and when these efforts don't persuade the parent, they are at a loss. Intimidating parents can make them defensive, can provoke them into making mistakes in meetings, and can ultimately run roughshod over them.

Even if they had a thirst for combat, most teachers rightly feel that they cannot respond angrily to these parents or answer their rudeness with rudeness. Consequently, they have few weapons with which to rebut accusations and defuse threats.

LOOKING AHEAD

We've concentrated on the 5 percenters because they exact such a heavy toll on schools. In so doing, we've repeated a pattern found universally in education, in many other spheres—and in life itself. A small minority of difficult challenges occupy a disproportionate amount of time and attention.

The good news is that schools are not helpless. Both the 95 and the 5 percenters can be worked with. In the third section of this book we describe ways to restructure the home-school partnership in order to strengthen overall cooperation and reduce conflict, ways to do constructive problem-solving with 95 percenters, and ways to minimize the negative impact of 5 percenters.

Although the proportions of 95 percenters and 5 percenters are undoubtedly similar for families of color, Black parents and their children encounter unique challenges in predominantly white schools with a predominantly white faculty.

It is important that we understand the different contexts and experiences these parents bring with them when they enroll their child in an independent school. The next chapter provides some insights we hope will help white teachers better support Black students and their parents.

ENDNOTES

[1] Johns Hopkins Medicine, "Mental Health Disorder Statistics," Johns Hopkins University; online at https://www.hopkinsmedicine.org/health/wellness-and-prevention/mental-health-disorder-statistics.

[2] National Institute of Mental Health, "Mental Illness"; online at https://www.nimh.nih.gov/health/statistics/mental-illness.shtml.

[3] Emily M. Douglas and David Finkelhor, "Childhood Sexual Abuse Fact Sheet," Crimes Against Children Research Center, University of New Hampshire, May 2005; online at http://unh.edu/ccrc/factsheet/pdf/childhoodSexualAbuseFactSheet.pdf.

It's vital for educators at predominantly white schools to understand the realities of the Black experience and strive to form better, more trusting relationships across racial lines.

Chapter 6

White Teachers and Black Families

Eighty percent of teachers in independent schools are white, while fewer than 7% of families are Black.[1] As a result, many teachers lack experience in working with Black families or are uncomfortable with addressing conflicts that arise on racial lines. Ideally, all teachers will develop broad cultural literacy so they can better understand families from a range of ethnic and national backgrounds. But in this chapter we are focusing on Black-white relationships because of the particular history of systemic racism in the United States as a whole and in schools in particular. That painful history can make conversations between white teachers and Black parents especially uncomfortable. It calls for educators to overcome their discomfort in order to fulfill the commitment to diversity, equity, and inclusion (DEI) that so many schools proclaim.

Howard Stevenson, the author of *Promoting Racial Literacy in Schools*, believes that for teachers to develop racial literacy requires a great deal of in-person practice as well as cognitive, behavioral, and emotional skill sets.[2] This is a large, complex undertaking that requires a comprehensive effort by an entire school, one that lies well beyond the scope of this book. In this chapter, we want to offer some immediate suggestions to help white teachers work with Black families. To communicate successfully with Black parents, we think white teachers must understand four realities about the Black experience in predominantly white schools. We also offer four actions teachers and schools can take to better communicate with the parents from these families.

FOUR REALITIES ABOUT THE BLACK EXPERIENCE IN PREDOMINANTLY WHITE SCHOOLS

Reality 1: Race is always in the room, and so-called color blindness doesn't work.

Rachel Jean-Baptiste, a mother and the director of diversity, equity, and inclusion at the King School (CT), is a Haitian American immigrant who describes herself as "a classic Caribbean immigrant parent in search of a quality educational experience" for her child. She describes herself as very dark-skinned and reports that when educators tell her "I don't see your color," she doesn't believe it; she experiences the speaker as disingenuous. Her internal reply is "If you don't see my Blackness, you don't see me."

As the mother of a multiracial child with much lighter skin than hers, Jean-Baptiste knows that colorism is a fact. All over the world, in countries like India and China or even in countries as diverse as Brazil, people have reactions and make judgments about others' worth and intelligence based on skin tones. To deny that reality is to be willfully naïve. If a teacher chooses to ignore the impact of color and race on a child's school experience and social life, and therefore on the parents' experience in the school, a Black parent will conclude that the teacher is clueless.

Robert Greene, an African American father and educator, reports that he often listens to tone and watches body language when a teacher says the word "Black" to get a sense of how comfortable the teacher is with discussing race. When his son was in first grade in an independent school, his closest friend was a boy, also Black, who left the school at the end of the year when his family moved away. This left Greene's son as the only Black boy in his grade, a situation that continued until sixth grade. No teacher or administrator ever proactively or independently mentioned the fact of his son's social position to Greene. If he brought it up, teachers would say, "I am so glad you mentioned *this*," as if it were an abstract subject. Greene's reaction was more personal: "You can't teach 'em unless you know 'em," he says, and a teacher not mentioning that his son was the only Black child in the class meant to him that the teacher did not understand fully the life his son was living in that school.

Greene finds that many white independent school teachers lack a "confident curiosity" about the experiences of Black children and their parents. Greene needs to know that his sons' teachers—he has two boys who have attended three different independent schools—are concerned about the boys' racial identity because that facet of their cultural identity will play a critical role in the quality of their experience. We heard from many Black parents that they have to provide a lot of identity support for their children when they attend a predominantly white school. They cannot trust that the teachers or the curriculum will support their children's pride in their own race.

Reality 2: Black parents can never fully trust their child's predominantly white school.

A group of fifth grade boys were taunting a group of their girl classmates at recess, using some raunchy and insulting words. It went on for some time until finally one of the teachers on recess duty had had enough. She walked over and, grabbing the shoulder of the only Black boy in the group, marched him publicly across the playground and into the office of the elementary school director for punishment. The other boys were relieved she hadn't chosen them but also a bit confused. They knew very well that he wasn't the ringleader. When the boy's parents heard about what had happened, they immediately labeled it as a "racial incident." The teacher denied that there was any racial basis to her action, and the head of school proclaimed, "We don't have racial incidents at our school." The father, an attorney, threatened to file suit in order to get the school's attention.

Black parents who send their children to independent schools want what all parents want: for their children to be known, to be cared about, and to be well-educated. They want their children to reach their full potential. In that regard, they share the hopes and dreams of all parents. What makes them different is that they can never trust that the school will not be unconsciously racist—because they have firsthand experience with precisely that. Stevenson says that the first thought that a Black parent has about enrolling at an independent school is "Are you going to hurt my child?"[3]

Most teachers would recoil at the very idea. In their minds, teachers are trustworthy. They are of good character, have good intentions, and would never knowingly hurt any child of any color. Because they so trust their own intentions and may be unaware of unconscious bias, teachers may not see the racial dimensions of the choices they make. They have a hard time imagining that their impact might miss the mark.

By contrast, it is not at all hard for Black parents to wonder whether they have put their child in harm's way by placing them in a predominantly white school. Black parents believe that, in school as in society, their child will frequently encounter small manifestations of racism (microaggressions) as well as larger, more overt racial prejudice and conflicts. Like all of the Black independent school alumni who shared stories of feeling unsafe by using the #Black@ hashtag in 2020, every Black parent we interviewed had at least one painful story of racial insensitivity in their child's school.

One mother reported that when her son was in fifth grade, a white boy transferred into the grade. Impulsive and provocative, the new boy tried to make his mark by using the N-word in reference to her son. And he didn't stop there; he was an equal opportunity insult specialist who pointed to some bird poop in the playground and told an Indian boy that it was the same color as his mother's skin.

The school's administrators were slow to react. Though they counseled the offending boy and eventually suspended him and required him to watch a cultural sensitivity video, his behavior never really changed. It was two full years before they dismissed him from the school. Though the other parents in the grade recognized the problem and rallied around the family of the racially targeted students to support them, in the end it was the administration's failure to move faster in a situation of overt racism that this Black mother remembers. "These schools can do tremendous things for children," she said, "and they can cause a lot of harm."

Reality 3: A teacher needs to be aware of both race and class issues.

In their attempts to diversify racially, large numbers of independent schools have reached out to recruit Black students, many of whom—though by no means all—come from families that cannot afford the school's tuition. Often, the schools have raised funds or reached into their endowment to support Black students they have recruited. But as eager as they may be to diversify, too many schools, in our view, don't attend to the kinds of transitions and sacrifices a family and a student may have to make to join the school. These can sometimes begin at the most basic level, with transportation, if, say, the family lives in an urban area and the school is located far away in a suburb. And some of the painful feelings that students of color on financial aid experience come from white students' casual comments about money, expensive clothes, and vacations rather than race. An educator who is not attuned to issues of socioeconomic inequality and the impact they can have on children may miss an important part of what this means to a student's experience at the school.

Teachers may need to be sensitive to the fact of one Black child's relatively low family income, but they cannot assume that color and low socioeconomic status necessarily go together. They need to be aware that Black students may come from families of considerable means. Teachers who assume that the Black children in their classes are, by virtue of their skin color, on financial aid and who therefore make assumptions about their parents' lack of education may be surprised and embarrassed to find themselves talking to Black physicians, business executives, professors, and the like. We can assure you: These parents will register a teacher's assumptions and condescension because they have experienced such treatment before.

Schools often feel that they are protecting families by withholding information about which children are on scholarship, and there may be truth to that. However, teachers cannot be aware of issues of race and class if they don't have some data. It is the responsibility of administrators to keep their teachers aware and informed so they can fully understand the experience of a Black child in their school, whether the student is affluent or not.

Reality 4: Teachers need to see their curriculum through a racial lens.

Teachers are often deeply attached to their curricula; language teachers love the books they teach and do not want to give up the experience of sharing them with their students. For example, *Johnny Tremain* has long been a late elementary or middle school classic, a historical novel of the American Revolution that many former students cherish in their memories. However, the book includes a scene in which an enslaved woman accidentally throws water on Johnny's feet. He berates her and warns her that if he had more time, he could indict her entire race. Like *Johnny Tremain*, once-beloved books such as *The Witch of Blackbird Pond* that use Black people simply as props and stories that refer to Native Americans as "savages" need to be reevaluated, taught very differently, or discarded.

But it isn't simply the classics that need reevaluation through a racial lens. All teachers have to ask themselves: Can a Black child or any child of color in my class ever see his or her life mirrored in my curriculum?

Black parents told us stories of teachers who consider themselves so "woke" or post-racial that in class they read aloud sections of *Huck Finn* and *To Kill a Mockingbird* that contain the N-word. One teacher even gave a passage containing the N-word to a Black student to read aloud. The boy felt ashamed and devastated by the experience; the teacher did not see it. Should a teacher make that kind of decision without consulting other teachers, a DEI director, or the parents of the Black children in that classroom? We think not.

Robert Smith, a Black graduate of an independent school in Minneapolis, recalled loving to sing when he was a fourth grader. He also loved his music teacher and wanted very much to please her. With a talent show coming up, and apparently without any awareness of the controversy around DuBose Heyward and Ira Gershwin's "Black" lyrics, his teacher scheduled him to sing "I Got Plenty O' Nuttin'" from *Porgy and Bess*. It was the only song like it in the talent show, and it was completely without context.

When Smith's mother heard about the song Robert had been given, she was furious. She went to the school and demanded that the teacher change his song, which the teacher did. Like many children, Smith was upset that his mother had made trouble with his teacher. Looking back, he thinks he didn't experience any hurt by the teacher's song choice, but he realizes that his mother was put in a terrible position by having to be the "angry Black mother." After that incident, his parents were always more vigilant and mistrustful of the school, showing that a teacher can sometimes keep an alliance with the child while losing the parents' trust.

FOUR ACTIONS WHITE TEACHERS CAN TAKE TO STRENGTHEN RELATIONSHIPS WITH BLACK PARENTS

In the wake of the racial reckoning that swept across America in 2020, many schools have realized the need for a process of sustained systemic change, one that will extend over years, not months. The nature and extent of this effort in each individual school will shape the specific context of relationships between white teachers and Black parents and students.

As part of this larger effort, we have four specific suggestions we believe will help teachers form better, more trusting relationships across racial lines. The first suggestion concerns asking questions. That's because, as psychologists, we believe that there are fundamental ways to connect with other human beings, and being curious about them is the best possible start. However, when there are tensions and potential barriers to connection, such as race and socioeconomic differences, a bit more courage is required on the part of the questioner. Many of the things we suggest will take practice on the part of teachers, as well as a willingness to make mistakes.

Suggestion 1: Ask questions—in particular "hopes and fears" questions as they relate to the school and to race.

A young white teacher once asked us how she could convince Black parents that she was alert to the issues of racism; she wanted them to know that she was personally inspired by the Black Lives Matter movement, she had read a lot about anti-racism, and she had been examining her curriculum closely.

Our answer to her was that she should not take up parents' time with assurances about how anti-racist she was. What teachers need to do is convey that they want to learn about the parents and their child and that they are comfortable talking about race. Teachers do that by asking three types of questions: hopes, fears, and racial identity.

- **"Hopes" questions:** Whenever teachers have a chance to talk with the parents of a Black child in their class, they should ask questions about how the family learned about the school, why they chose it, and what they were hoping for in terms of academic achievement as well as extracurricular experiences. Even if a teacher cannot deliver on a parent's every hope—no teacher can promise to do so—it is important to hear his or her aspirations. Then, teachers should ask about the child's previous school experience and whether the child was excited about the move. ("Where did your child go before ABC Academy?" "Did your child want to leave the old school?" "What is the child hoping for here?") We have met a number of Black children who say bluntly that they didn't want to come to an independent school. This is important for the teacher to know.

- **"Fears" questions:** A teacher can always ask any parent, "Is there anything you're worried about with respect to your child's education?" But if Black parents don't raise any issue about their child being in a minority, the teachers need to address it, asking, for example, "Do you have any worries about your child entering ABC Academy? About this being a predominantly white school?" "Has your child encountered racism in the previous school setting? I want to make my students' experience the best it can be, so I invite you to share any fears or concerns you may have at any time so that I can address them."

  Then the teacher needs to listen and ask intelligent follow-up questions that go to the specifics of the fears. In the "toolkit" chapters, we will discuss the power of "hopes and fears" questions in greater detail. For the moment, we want to point out that we have never encountered a parent of color who didn't appreciate and want to answer the question, "Do you have any worries about having chosen a predominantly white school for your child?" It opens doors.

- **"Racial identity" questions:** The most effective way to let Black parents know that the teacher is going to pay attention to what happens to their child's racial identity at a predominantly white school is to ask directly about it. Do the parents have fears about their child's social life in this school? Are the parents doing anything outside of school to support their child's racial identity, for example, through a Black youth group at church? If so, the teacher would like to know about that.

The most frequent complaint we have heard from Black students over the years, particularly from those on financial aid, is that "they"—white students and white teachers—aren't interested in or curious about the Black students' lives. When Black parents meet with a teacher, the teacher's confident curiosity in asking about their family, their experience beyond the school, and, most important, any racial concerns they may have can help build an alliance with the family. By saying "confident" here we don't mean "intrusive" or "overweening" but "respectfully direct." Building this confidence requires practice and is greatly helped when the school itself has a sincere commitment to racial literacy.

Suggestion 2: Be willing to offer straight talk.

Randall Dunn, the head of the Latin School of Chicago, who is Black, says that some white teachers are sometimes less than candid with Black parents about their child's academic performance and difficulties. Perhaps the teachers are trying to soften the pain of telling Black parents that their child isn't keeping up with other students or needs some support and accommodations. The fear of expressing a racial stereotype might be stressful for teachers. But teachers need to remember that the academic gaps between white and Black students in the United States, in both public and independent schools, are well-documented by research. These facts are not a secret. Black parents know very well that for a multitude of reasons—including deficits in preparation, difficulties in transportation, social dislocation, and the racial stereotyping a child may experience—their child may struggle.

We believe that it is never a mistake to tell any parent "I am worried about your child" because it is evidence of caring. However, the stress of speaking across racial lines is real. So if a white teacher feels uncomfortable about telling parents that their child is struggling academically and doesn't know how to speak straightforwardly about it, it is always possible to frame the issue as a question or series of questions: "Is your son saying anything about his math homework?" "Does your son talk about his difficulties with math?" "Are you aware that he is feeling overwhelmed?"

Once parents get to say that they do, indeed, see the child's struggles, then a more straightforward conversation is possible. Delicate, euphemistic, and avoidant conversations are no help to anyone, least of all the child.

Suggestion 3: Provide equal discipline.

Black students make up only 16% of students in American public schools, yet they receive 40% of school suspensions.[4] Research has documented the racial disproportionality in school discipline over decades; these disparities necessarily make Black parents worry that their child will not be treated fairly, even in an independent school. They may especially worry for their sons because they know that Black boys are more easily stereotyped as disruptive and dangerous, although evidence shows that Black girls suffer similarly unfair treatment compared to white girls.[5]

Therefore, when a teacher disciplines a Black student, the situation can be fraught; it can test the relationship between teacher and parents. However, to choose not to discipline a Black student who requires some limits is a disservice both to the child and to the class. It is vital that teachers keep an eye on their disciplinary decisions to make sure that they are not affected by race. It might be helpful to check with a colleague or the school's director of diversity, equity, and inclusion to see whether the decisions strike them as even-handed.

A veteran middle school teacher who is white told us that although he had participated in many anti-racist discussion groups and was steadily growing more comfortable with racial issues, he faced a problem with a Black eighth grade boy who was athletic, physically large, charismatic, and socially powerful. The teacher saw him as being "mean" to other students and reported this to his mother. She responded that she found the teacher unsupportive compared to her son's seventh grade teacher, who had been an advocate for the boy. While they never talked about race directly, she clearly disqualified the teacher on what felt to him like racial grounds. However, he was not able to take up that issue with her directly. His relationship with the mother never healed after that. He was left doubting himself and wondering what else he might have done to effectively convey his concerns to the mother.

A few years later, in another school, that same teacher had a Black seventh grade boy who was constantly breaking small rules. Whenever the teacher tried to hold the boy accountable, the boy would tell him, "You're racist." His answer would be, "Well, maybe I am. Let's go talk to the DEI director and let him assess the situation." The two of them would go together and lay out the facts. The DEI director, who was Black, regularly found that the boy was—surprise, surprise—a standard-issue, annoying seventh grade boy interested in pushing any and all limits. Eventually, after numerous arbitrations, the boy stopped making the "racist" accusations, and the teacher and he formed a close bond.

We cannot offer white teachers a simple formula for disciplining Black students. Disciplinary situations across racial lines always have the potential to be difficult and there is no panacea. Obviously, it helps to have an educator of color involved in the decision-making process. But the criteria for good discipline are really common sense: fairness, proportionality, precedent, and, when the situation is serious, a genuine effort to involve the parents in the discussions from the beginning. And, as uncomfortable as it may be, it can help to ask the parents whether they are experiencing the discipline as having a racial dimension.

Suggestion 4: Reach out, reach out, reach out.

When we interviewed Black parents and educators for this chapter, their number one suggestion for schools to improve relationships was "Reach out"—take the initiative to make Black parents feel included. A number of the examples above illustrate ways that individual teachers can do this, but the school leaders and parents we interviewed emphasized that teachers' individual efforts can never be enough. Nor is it enough to modify the curriculum, though this, too, is important. Above all, the school culture must become more inclusive. The goal is not just to make Black families feel they are welcome in the school but to make it clear that the school belongs to them as much as it does to everyone else.

A white head of school told us that although students of color now constitute more than 30% of his school, he believes that almost none of those students' parents feel as if the school is truly theirs, too. Other heads we talked to agreed. This problem is reflected in many ways.

For example, many heads have told us that when their school's parent association presents the names of candidates for officers, usually none are parents of color. This is not necessarily a surprise because few Black parents regularly attend P.A. events. Too often, this may be because there has often been a polite but perfunctory outreach to Black parents rather than a genuine invitation to participate in the life of the school. A willingness to inquire about what would make participation easier is in order.

Another example comes from a white head of school who observed that it is largely white parents who feel "privileged" to voice concerns. By comparison, he said, Black parents "complain too little; they don't bring up issues because they don't want to raise racial tensions or make white teachers feel uncomfortable." They haven't been sufficiently encouraged to let their voices be heard. It is essential, he believes, for white educators to reach out to Black parents to find out what they are feeling about their child's experience.

Randall Dunn agrees that Black parents are "daunted by the potential of being accused of playing the race card." As a veteran educator and school head, he observes that for Black families, "when you get in, it's like you won the lottery, and when things start to go bad, it's like they are taking your winnings away." He grew up in a low-income Boston neighborhood and received a scholarship to attend Milton Academy, which was geographically nearby but socioeconomically "worlds apart." In Dunn's case, outreach did much to bridge the gap and make his school years a success. He received a number of awards at Milton, and a white teacher who connected with him made sure that his mother could attend the various ceremonies. The teacher also offered to arrange for him to become a boarding student, if he wished. Dunn did, which, he says, "made a huge difference in my life."

Kai Bynum remembers that when he was the director of community and diversity at Belmont Hill School, a ninth grade boy began to spiral downward academically. Bynum wanted to be in contact with the boy's mother and kept leaving her voice messages encouraging her to keep the school informed of what was going on. She didn't. He knew from the boy that his mother had had a history of substance abuse problems, and he guessed that both she and the boy were depressed. He called the mother and invited her to his office. She was just unable to cross the lines of race and class to come to the fancy campus of a predominantly white school. So he met with her in a coffee shop near her home to try to establish an alliance. "You need to trust me," Bynum said, "and we need to be a team." Finally, he convinced her to come to campus and meet with him and her son. The boy was furious that Mr. Bynum had brought his mother onto campus; like many adolescents, he wanted his worlds kept separate. Nevertheless, the intervention worked. The boy started doing his academic work again, and his grades went up. He stayed and graduated.

Many educators told us stories of Black students, particularly boys, who start to "disappear" during their school careers. One boy, who had never been a strong student in an academically demanding, predominantly white school, had been subtly withdrawing since the beginning of 11th grade. He was admitted to college in the fall of his senior year and after that appeared to be even less engaged. When the coronavirus pandemic hit in 2020 and the school went online, he completely fell off the screen, literally. He did not attend Zoom classes or turn in work. His teachers left him email messages and tried to call his cellphone. He did not respond to any of them.

Finally, the Black director of diversity, equity, and inclusion became so worried that he left the home where he was sequestered, put on a mask, and drove to the boy's house and knocked on the door. When they were face-to-face, he asked the boy, "Do you want to graduate?" The boy nodded yes, and the DEI director said, "Well, then you have to answer my calls."

Two days later he received a phone call from the boy's mother, who opened up and began to sob. Her son had been considered a talented student at his previous school, she said, but when he started at his new independent school in ninth grade, he suddenly experienced himself as a mediocre performer. That loss of identity and confidence had grown increasingly severe over his years at the school. His pride and shame had kept him from telling anyone until he essentially dropped out and almost failed to graduate. Yet his mother had known the story all along. Why hadn't someone at the school heard that story about his loss of confidence a year or two earlier? Had the mother avoided coming to the school? Had no one been comfortable telling her that her son was disengaged from the community?

We asked the DEI director, "Could a white teacher have successfully connected with him in the way you did? Did it have to be a Black man?" He replied, "Actually, the boy's adviser, who is white, had been seriously considering going over to his house." But he didn't go. Something, perhaps fear of making a mistake, made the adviser hesitate to reach out, and the DEI director got there first.

As we said earlier, outreach is a vital part of an inclusive school culture. Just as there is every reason for schools to recruit Black professionals to the teaching and administrative ranks, it is also reasonable to assume that white teachers and Black students can forge meaningful relationships, and that white educators can become strong, effective advocates for students across racial lines.

ENDNOTES

[1] NAIS, Data and Analysis for School Leadership (DASL), "Facts at a Glance, 2019-20"; online at https://www.nais.org/getmedia/cb3cbc7a-a703-43b9-9091-3680b66c782c/2019-20-Facts-at-a-Glance-(NAIS-Members).pdf.

[2] Howard C. Stevenson, *Promoting Racial Literacy in Schools: Differences That Make a Difference* (New York: Teachers College Press, 2014).

[3] Ibid.

[4] Nora Gordon, "Disproportionality in Student Discipline: Connecting Policy to Research," Brookings Institution, January 2018; online at https://www.brookings.edu/research/disproportionality-in-student-discipline-connecting-policy-to-research/.

[5] Monique Morris, *Pushout: The Criminalization of Black Girls in Schools* (New York: The New Press, 2016); online at https://clcjbooks.rutgers.edu/books/pushout-the-criminalization-of-black-girls-in-schools/. Kimberlé Williams Crenshaw with Priscilla Ocen and Jyoti Nanda, "Black Girls Matter: Pushed Out, Overpoliced, and Underprotected," African American Policy Forum and Center for Intersectionality and Social Policy Studies, 2015; online at https://static1.squarespace.com/static/53f20d90e4b0b80451158d8c/t/54dcc1ece4b001co 3e323448/1423753708557/AAPF_BlackGirlsMatterReport.pdf.

The standard ways of building parent cooperation aren't working, and when finances get tight, schools may be inadvertently fostering attitudes and expectations that undermine the home-school partnership.

Chapter 7

The Old Approach, A New Crunch

For decades, schools have looked to resolve problems with parents in two ways: individually and institutionally.

The individual approach is situational and reactive; teachers and administrators respond to each episode as it arises, using whatever skills they have developed to resolve the situation and, perhaps, to make it a teachable moment.

The institutional approach is systemic and, ideally, preventive; it operates at the schoolwide level and aims to reduce and avert problem behavior, chiefly through educational programs for parents.

Most schools still rely primarily on the first approach, and, when they see the need, they supplement their efforts with the second. It's a model that may have worked well enough back when schools enjoyed much higher levels of institutional authority than they now do. But it is no longer effective, both because of the parental anxieties and behaviors we've outlined and because many schools, faced with serious enrollment and financial challenges, are unintentionally exacerbating the very trends in parent behavior that they find so troublesome.

THE STANDARD APPROACH: PARENT EDUCATION

Let's start with this example. A senior receives a D in English for the fall term after failing to hand in two major papers and being caught plagiarizing on another. His parents rally to his defense. They attack the teacher as incompetent and unfair, insist that their son didn't really plagiarize, and accuse the teacher of damaging the boy's college admission prospects. They demand that his grade be changed. The teacher tries, in vain, to defend himself but ends up frustrated and unhappy.

In follow-up meetings, the dean of studies and the division head defend the teacher. They try to persuade the parents that neither the teacher nor the school would ever mistreat students, that there is an important life lesson for the boy to learn, that it's important for the school and parents to find common ground, and that the grade will not be changed. The parents eventually accept the decision, but they aren't happy about it.

It is important to note here that none of the three educators is a beginner and that all have dealt with parents for years. However, none has received any special training for situations like this. The whole incident has cost them significant stress, time, and energy, and it hasn't improved the parents' fundamental outlook or their relationship with the school.

Now let's say that several roughly similar incidents occur in other grades or courses, or that, more generally, parent attitudes toward, and treatment of, faculty become less respectful and more antagonistic. Administrators and teachers realize that just responding in turn to each episode means that they will always be putting out fires, never preventing them. So they decide to be proactive. They try to educate parents, hoping that information and guidance will improve parents' perspective on their children, their willingness to let students learn from the consequences of their actions, and their respect for the school itself. This approach generally consists of evening talks or workshops, sometimes in a series but more often on an occasional basis. Sometimes the sessions are presented by school staff, other times by outside experts. The school team arranges a program, or a series of them, on developmental topics such as

"Raising Today's Adolescent" or "Strengthening the Home-School Partnership."

For 40 years, we have each participated in and consulted about these kinds of programs. In that time, as we've said, the knowledge base about child and adolescent development has grown significantly, as have the number of guidance counselors and school psychologists and the sophistication of their training.

But none of this has strengthened the impact of the parent education programs schools offer. Even when the program is well received by those who attend, the school rarely sees the kind of change it seeks.

The problem with relying on these kinds of programs begins at the most basic level, with attendance. Parents are ever busier, their time consumed by the demands of work, of transporting children to multiple sports and other activities, and so on. They are less and less likely to come to a program, especially a series of them. For years now, schools across the country have been reporting that audiences have been waning. Worse, the parents who, in the school's view, most need the programs typically attend them least. In fact, the audiences tend to consist largely of the school's most supportive mothers. We remember the guidance counselor who told us:

> We're always preaching to the choir, and mainly the sopranos and altos. I'd like to send a special notice to our most difficult and most ineffective parents, including the dads: *We planned this evening specifically for you. Be here or else!* I keep hoping, but they rarely come.

And although it is difficult to fill an auditorium for a topic on child or adolescent development, it is impossible to do so for a program about improving the home-school relationship. These usually draw only the most devoted members of the school's parents association, and virtually no fathers.

Two substantive issues also limit the impact of these programs. One is the amount of misinformation many parents have absorbed from advice books, as noted in Chapter 4. They need more of the most basic kind of information and assistance, which makes it hard to cover an adequate amount of information in an evening.

Another is the very nature of parenting: It lends itself poorly to advice. It is so involving, touches so many parts of a person that are emotional rather than purely rational, and does so with such immediacy that it is hard to do planfully. It's one thing to contemplate in an evening workshop ways to de-escalate the tantrums of an oppositional teenager. It's quite another to actually do so in the heat of the moment at home, when feelings and frustration are running high and when it is the fourth tantrum of the week.

To be clear, there is no reason for schools to stop offering parent education. But, in our view, schools need to moderate their expectations about the outcomes. These programs do, indeed, preach to the choir. That's what they're good at. It's a valid, useful function. It helps the choir stay in tune. It encourages parents who have good childrearing judgment to trust that judgment and act on it—and to trust the school.

But these programs are *not* a vehicle for significantly changing parents' behavior, especially the behavior of those who are most problematic. These parents are not just the least likely to attend. They are also the least likely to be persuaded by a 90-minute presentation to change the way they treat their children—and the school. Solid, informative parent education programming can be a helpful support to a school's partnership with parents, but such programming is not the partnership's cornerstone.

THE NEW CRUNCH IN ENROLLMENT AND FINANCE

Since 2008, the standard approach has been weakened in another significant way. Although educators focus on what they see as negative changes among parents, the harsh realities of the post-financial-meltdown context schools inhabit have led many of them to be complicit in these very changes, enabling some of the very behaviors schools find most problematic. Large numbers of schools now live in a new and much more fraught world that began with the Great Recession of 2007 to 2009. It's hard to remember now, but throughout the 1990s and into the 2000s, a top issue in the independent school world was managing growth. Established schools were expanding, new schools were opening, tuition increases kept outpacing inflation, but applications kept rising and attrition was low. Schools were enjoying what former NAIS President Patrick Bassett called the luxury of higher enrollments and higher prices.[1]

The financial meltdown shattered this era of growth. Schools suddenly had to start managing austerity and retrenchment. Even though the economy had recovered in most parts of the U.S. by 2017, anxiety about—and threats to—enrollment and finance caused sustained hardship for many schools, threatened the viability of others, and made many schools reluctant to be assertive with parents. The COVID-19 pandemic that began in early 2020 did nothing to ease the problem and much to exacerbate it.

An NAIS survey of 800 independent schools found that between 2013-2014 and 2017-2018, 64% of elementary schools and 51% of elementary/middle schools lost enrollment. Things were better, though hardly robust, among K-12 schools, where just less than half (45%) lost enrollment. Pure upper schools fared best, although 30% still reported a decline.[2] Admissions officers point to a range of factors that caused enrollment to drop. These include a decline in the school-age population in parts of the country; an overhang of anxiety from the Great Recession that made parents hesitant about tuition commitments; a rising proportion of parents who are millennials and less secure financially than preceding generations; and competition from charter schools, for-profit schools, and home schooling.[3]

Fifty-five percent of schools received fewer applications in 2017-2018 than they did 10 years earlier, and nearly one-third saw a decline of 20% or more. Particularly ominous is that the falloff in lower school enrollment has been accelerating and fed by double-digit drops in kindergarten and first and second grades, where application levels are lowest and attrition levels highest.[4]

Whatever the causes, when enrollment is under pressure, so, inevitably, is finance. Most schools lack large endowments and are highly tuition dependent. For them, the luxury of strong admissions, now long gone, took with it the luxury of strong budgets. The net effect has been to weaken the schools' position vis à vis their "customers"—especially in schools where the supply of seats outstrips demand. In their efforts to cope, many schools have naturally become less selective and are fully enrolled only because they've expanded their admissions criteria. They now admit students they formerly would not have accepted.

Often, this includes those with moderate or more serious learning disabilities, even if the school has little experience with such students and its faculty is unprepared to teach them. If, as too frequently happens, the school doesn't train its teachers or hire faculty with special education expertise, the students begin falling behind their classmates—a formula for distressing their parents and increasing the likelihood of hostile interactions.

Other schools are full only because they now discount tuition for some families who don't actually qualify for financial aid but who won't enroll their children unless they receive a tuition reduction. From the very get-go, these parents have reason to see their relationship with the school as transactional and to feel that they hold the upper hand vis à vis the school.

In addition to modifying admission and tuition standards, a great many schools have responded to the post-2008 enrollment/finance threats by boosting their marketing. (The years after the Great Recession were a boom time for branding consultants.) Even the smallest schools now make big claims in their mission and vision statements and their viewbooks; none want to be outpromised.

This emphasis has been accompanied by an enhanced customer service orientation that can further encourage the most consumerist tendencies of parents. In addition to marketing themselves aggressively, many now survey parents more frequently to assess their satisfaction. As the late Claudia Daggett, former executive director of the Independent Schools Association of the Central States, pointed out, this can contribute to a "Yelp effect." It encourages parents to treat their relationship with the school in precisely the entitled, transactional ways that can cause the school such distress.[5]

THE NEED FOR A DIFFERENT APPROACH

All this can leave schools over a barrel when it comes to managing effective relationships with parents—and maintaining appropriate boundaries. Educators apprehensive about enrollment and finance can't help worrying about losing customers. This can make them hesitant to defend their values and policies, reluctant to resist parental demands for special treatment, scared to speak frankly about what will best serve students.

At a meeting of division heads from smaller schools, there was broad agreement when one said, "If we have a really tough set of parents, it's always in the back of our minds that they could pull their child if they become too unhappy with us. If they're full-pay, we're extra anxious." As they talked, the group acknowledged that the old ways of building parent cooperation weren't working and that their schools had been inadvertently fostering in parents the very attitudes and expectations that undermine an effective home-school partnership.

"We need," said another division head, "a new approach to all this."

ENDNOTES

[1] Patrick Bassett, "Financing Independent Schools for the 21st Century," *Independent School* magazine, Fall 2003; online at https://www.nais.org/magazine/independent-school/fall-2003/financing-independent-schools-for-the-21st-century/.

[2] Joseph Corbett and Myra McGovern, "The Enrollment Outlook," *2018-2019 NAIS Trendbook* (Washington, DC: NAIS, 2018), pp. 43, 49.

[3] Joseph Corbett and Amada Torres, "The Enrollment Outlook," *2019-2020 NAIS Trendbook* (Washington, DC: NAIS, 2019), pp. 18-25.

[4] Ibid.

[5] Claudia Daggett, "Out the Door: What We Can Learn from Abrupt Departures from Headship," *The Trustee's Letter*, June 2018; online at https://resources.finalsite.net/images/v1565972701/isacsorg/jy8tbj9sniaum6lultva/DaggettC_Outthedoor_TheTrusteessLetterIndependentThinkingJune2018_1.pdf.

PART 3

COPING

Fortunately, there are practical ways for schools to resolve or, better yet, prevent communication problems with parents.

■

Schools can assume the role of senior partner in the home-school relationship by clarifying two key facets of school life: purpose and conduct.

Chapter 8

Restructuring the Partnership

I n our experience, the schools that encounter the fewest boundary-breaking problems and preserve the best relationships with their families begin at the systemic, not the situational, level. These schools treat the shifts in parent behavior as the new normal, not an aberrant pendulum swing. They don't anticipate a return to the levels of respect, trust, cooperation, and confidence schools once enjoyed. Instead, they work to redefine the home-school partnership as one in which the school is the senior partner. In so doing, these schools counter a pronounced trend in American education toward treating parents as coequals in the enterprise of schooling. A message many schools repeat is "Parents know their children best." Of course, parents *do* know their children better and more fully than educators can. But what matters is not just knowing a child best but knowing what's best for a child—particularly at school. And here the concept of an equal partnership falters.

As we have noted, parents' confidence and childrearing competence are both diminishing; so is their direct engagement in their children's lives.

Moreover, most parents, even those with graduate degrees, are generally not well-informed about current educational realities. Their memories from their own school years lead them to underestimate how much more intricate classroom life has become and how much more complex it is to work with some of today's students.

An equal partnership between home and school still makes sense in terms of, say, aspiration—wanting the very best outcome for a student. But, as earlier chapters have shown, many parents who love their children deeply and want the best for them lack the developmental and educational savvy to be equal partners about their child's schooling.

Being the senior partner means that the school undertakes a systematic effort to build and sustain clarity throughout the school community about two key facets of school life: *purpose*, meaning core values; and *conduct*, or basic responsibilities. It means providing clear guidelines for parents about how best to interact with the school. In key ways, it means becoming more parental vis à vis parents—not by telling them how to parent but by modeling effective parenting in dealings with them. It absolutely does *not* mean condescending to parents, failing to listen to them, or dismissing their legitimate concerns. It means being appropriately, assertively clear about the school's values and expectations; about the boundaries of acceptable behavior; and about how disagreements and conflicts are handled.

CLARIFYING TWO FACETS OF SCHOOL LIFE

In the following pages, we describe how these two facets of school life—purpose and conduct—can be used to shape a healthy parent-school relationship.

Purpose: What We're All About

By purpose, we don't mean a standard school mission or vision statement. Although these are typically well-meant, most fail to inspire faculty. Indeed, in our experience, it's rare to find teachers who can even recite their school's mission or vision—in good part because the statements tend to be too long and to make pledges the school can't possibly fulfill. We certainly agree that schools should be aspirational, but we have almost never seen these statements capture the imagination in a serious way that shapes behavior.

Purpose, to us, means guiding principles: the school's core defining beliefs that mark its approach to students and teaching. Achieving clarity of purpose requires coalescing around a few truly central values, not a list of platitudes. These values are closer to a motto than to a typical mission or vision statement. A motto is simple and easy to remember; clear, yet adaptable; direct, yet general enough to be applied with some flexibility. The point is not that every school should have one but that every school should have a direct, fundamental sense of purpose. In most schools, purpose tends to center on academic excellence and values that come under the heading of respect for others, ethical responsibility, and the like. (The commitment to diversity, equity, and inclusion falls under values.) The values themselves vary among schools. What matters is building clarity and consensus about them.

One of the best examples we've ever encountered came from The Town School, a progressive pre-K-8 school in New York City. After prospective parents toured the school, Joyce Evans (no relation), then Town's head, would tell them:

> What you just saw on this tour is what you would get, and if this is right for your child, we'd love to have you apply. If not, there are many excellent schools in New York to consider. Your children may thrive in many school environments, but you may not. You need to trust the school, its philosophy, and those who lead.

If parents were seeking a quiet school, she would explain, "This may not be the school for you. As you can see, we have a hum." (The school did indeed have a hum; not a disorganized, chaotic noisiness but a lively, purposeful buzz.) "If you want your child always reading *at* a desk and never *under* a desk," she would add, "don't apply here. As you can see, some of our young children read under the desk."

By saying these things, Evans didn't mean that a hum and reading under the desk were themselves core values at Town, but that they exemplified the school's approach to education and its belief that young children learn best in a thoughtful but flexible creative environment. Her message on the school's website pointed to Town's motto, *Gaudeant Discentes* ("Let there be joy in learning") and described teachers at Town as "facilitators [who] orchestrate the productive 'hum' as students interact with one another, engage in discussions, use a myriad of resources and become involved in their own learning." Evans was determined that parents should know from the very outset what Town was—and what it wasn't.

Conduct: What It Means to Belong Here

Conduct refers to the way the school's core values are enacted and the conditions of membership in its community—that is, the *minimum nonnegotiables of belonging* to the school. Schools have no right to tell families how to live or what to believe, but schools cannot function without basic norms for behavior and basic shared understandings about education itself. And independent schools do have a right to lay out for parents—who, after all, are not forced to enroll their children—the core requirements of being part of the school community. Clarity regarding conduct is, at its heart, a commitment that a school's central values apply to its entire community: students, faculty, staff, administrators, trustees—and parents. Many schools have expectations for student behavior and a formal disciplinary code. The best have expectations for all their constituents.

Thus, if respect for others, say, is truly one of a school's core values, it's inadequate to simply teach this to students, expect them to demonstrate it, and acknowledge them when they do and correct them when they don't. The adults in the community—educators, staff, trustees, and parents alike—must also model respect and hold each other accountable for doing so. This has always been the primary way children learn values: through the example adults set more than the sermons they preach.

Some years ago, we began to encounter schools that had taken to spelling out expectations for parent conduct. Several had created formal documents parents had to sign. At Dwight-Englewood School (NJ), the late Jim Van Amburg, then head of school, developed a "values contract" that included three sections: "What the School Stands For," "What You Can Expect from the School," and "What the School Can Expect from You." A significant violation of its provisions by a student *or a parent* was grounds for not offering reenrollment for the next school year.

Invariably, these kinds of contracts were a response to episodes of extreme misbehavior. When Van Amburg described Dwight-Englewood's contract to a conference of school heads, he said, "I have three first-grade mothers on probation right now." They had been so outrageous toward teachers at the fall conference—pointing fingers and swearing at them, calling them names, and the like—that he had reminded the mothers that they had signed the contract. Although they were free to disagree with faculty, they could not do so disrespectfully, and any further episode would result in the school not offering enrollment the following year.

Van Amburg wasn't attacking these parents; he was defending his school's values. Of course, the parents felt criticized, and he was indeed confronting them, but his response was not ad hominem. It was undertaken in the name of shared community norms. He knew that a school can't defend what it hasn't proclaimed and there is little point in proclaiming what the school won't defend. No task is more important for a school leader than to be the voice of the school's covenant—to take primary responsibility for nourishing, celebrating, and protecting its core values and behavioral norms.

Few schools use a distinct values contract, but a great many have incorporated into their enrollment agreement language that confirms the importance of students *and* parents respecting the school's values. Often, the agreements state that failure to do so, by a student or a parent, could be grounds for separation from the school. Some of these documents contain explicit provisions, such as "I will abide by school rules and policies and will support the mission of the school" and "I will model appropriate ethical behavior for my children and others." Many schools don't go as far in this direction but do require parents and students to at least acknowledge in writing that they have read the school's handbook and the policies it contains.

The key is to build a broad, shared understanding about conduct among the larger school community. Student assemblies and all-school meetings, back-to-school nights, parent-teacher conferences, newsletters—all provide opportunities to underscore and reinforce core values. A startup initiative to increase awareness is not enough; there must be a continuing effort that includes orientation for new community members and reminders and refreshers for everyone. For students, these efforts can concentrate on values and behavior. For parents, it is often necessary to publish and reiterate very concrete guidelines about such things as how to communicate with the school.

Many schools now condense key guidelines and policies into a one-page summary and send it home several times a year (e.g., "Guidelines for Homework" and "How to Register a Concern"). In this regard, a special issue that plagues schools everywhere is parents' use of email and texting. The sheer volume of messages parents send, their impatience if they don't receive an immediate reply, the frequency with which their messages seek special treatment for their children and second-guess—or directly attack—teachers are all a source of distress and resentment among faculty. Most schools promise to return parents' messages within 24 hours but otherwise leave teachers on their own to cope. To uphold purpose and conduct, we strongly recommend a formal schoolwide policy like this:

> If you ever have a question or concern about your child, it is our policy to take questions or concerns directly to the faculty member involved, who will be in the best position to help sort things out. It is also our policy not to discuss any significant question or concern by email or text, as there is too much chance of unintentional miscommunication. To serve your children well, we need to understand one another clearly. If you send us such a message, you can expect a reply inviting you to set up a time to talk directly.

More schools now use back-to-school nights as opportunities to reiterate and reinforce these kinds of basics. Their essential message to parents: "To help your children grow up to be successful, these are the values and expectations we're teaching them. We need you to help us help them succeed by joining us as models of these values and behaviors."

Ideally, this message should begin early. A prospective family needs to know what kind of school it is joining, and the school needs to remember that it is welcoming a family, not just a student. Too many schools have decided that true excellence means being all things to all people. They neglect to prepare students and parents for what the school expects. Having failed to establish guidelines about community membership, they risk having their decisions, notably those about discipline, seen as arbitrary and capricious.

By contrast, the more clearly and energetically a school stands for something, the more attractive it proves to be—and the better prepared it is to hold all its members to its standards. This calls for exploring the goodness of fit between a family's expectations and the school's before admitting even the most promising student. Orientation programs should include an effort not just to make newcomers feel comfortable but also to be sure they are informed about "what it means to be part of us" as well as "what makes us, us."

It would be ideal if a school only had to do this once. Unfortunately, the challenge of orienting and informing parents is perpetual. Almost as soon as a school develops a cadre of informed, knowledgeable parents, it begins to lose them as their children move up through the grades and graduate. The process has to start all over again. But with repetition over time, the messages become embedded in the school's culture and are increasingly seen, and accepted, by incoming parents as "the way the school does things."

THE FACULTY ROLE

In our experience, teachers readily agree that their school should be appropriately prescriptive about the minimum nonnegotiables of the home-school partnership. Often, however, they are reluctant to accept these same conditions themselves. It is not enough for the administration to publish and proclaim guidelines if faculty implement them indifferently or ignore them altogether.

Independent schools are not just independent as organizations; they are also full of independent people who are typically allowed broad autonomy—autonomy they treasure. A simple example: In every secondary school that has a student uniform or dress code, there are teachers—often a great many—who don't enforce the standard and are allowed to get away with not enforcing it. In these schools, teachers—including those who disregard the requirement—complain about parents who let their children come to school ignoring it. But the message from the school itself is, at best, mixed, so it's not surprising that parents and students don't respect the school's policy.

Student dress may not seem to be a major issue; we use it only as an example. To the extent that a school is serious about restructuring its partnership with parents, it will need to think carefully about its most important minimum nonnegotiables and engage faculty in discussions to clarify the ways these key essentials apply to them, not just to students and parents. To name other examples: If the school has a policy about how much homework is assigned in middle school, it needs to be sure that all teachers respect this policy. And if the school has a commitment to diversity, equity, and inclusion, it needs to be sure that all faculty are educated appropriately and prepared to model this commitment in their dealings with one another, with students, and with parents.

All of this may be logical, but it swims against a strong cultural tide in schools. Although we have each consulted in hundreds of independent schools, we have encountered only a tiny few where a teacher who disregards a major institutional priority suffers any real consequence. Changing this culture of avoidance is a large task and beyond our scope here. But it can be done, and, in addition to helping reshape the home-school partnership, it will bring many other benefits.[1]

COHERENCE, NOT RIGIDITY

A focus on purpose and conduct may strike some as potentially narrow and suffocating, but its aim is to renew schools' institutional authority and organizational coherence, not to straitjacket anyone. It does not, for example, contradict a school's commitment to diversity, equity, and inclusion. Clarifying expectations for a heterogeneous group is much more complex than for a homogeneous one, so schools need to think especially hard about two things: the ways a school must adapt to the values and traditions of all the different families who join it and the common expectations (remember, the *minimum nonnegotiables*) the school must require of all participants in order to remain a coherent community.

In our view, purpose and conduct call for schools to hold fast to their core values *and* to reach out and adapt to their constituents.

ENDNOTE

[1] See Robert Evans, "Getting to No: Building True Collegiality in Schools," *Independent School* magazine, Winter 2012; online at https://www.nais.org/magazine/independent-school/winter-2012/getting-to-no/.

■

By adopting the right mindset and skills, schools can engage constructively with 95% of parents in service of their children.

Chapter 9

The Basic Toolkit

A school that works to restructure its partnership with families and clarify purpose and conduct will prevent many difficult encounters with parents and make others easier to resolve. But it can't eliminate them all. Not nearly, given that many challenges parents present are rooted in factors beyond the school's—and often beyond the parents'—control. So teachers and administrators need a toolkit to help them manage and resolve the inevitable difficulties that arise.

This chapter outlines essentials that we have found, over many years in many schools, to be helpful. Most are simple, though not always easy; some are obvious but hard to remember. We begin by suggesting a three-point mindset for dealing with parents and then offer five essential skills to manage the relationship. Altogether, these points form a solid foundation for building connection, resolving conflict, and restoring confidence.

THREE PRODUCTIVE WAYS TO THINK ABOUT WORKING WITH PARENTS

Educators need to approach the parent-teacher encounter with three assumptions.

Assumption 1: Parents are sincere and—especially important to remember—anxious.

Parents deserve the benefit of the doubt; they have to be seen as having a genuine concern for their child, even if their views seem exaggerated or entirely wrong. Sincerity is no guarantee of accuracy—a father's assessment of a situation may be wildly incorrect, which can make it hard to see that he means well, especially if his tone becomes negative, hostile, or demanding. In our experience, it is easy for teachers to give difficult students the benefit of the doubt but harder for them to do the same for parents. Remembering that the father's impulse to defend or advocate for his child is likely sincere can make it easier to tolerate his negativity and to seek common ground with him.

Even more important than assuming parents are sincere is to assume they're anxious. No matter how assertive they may seem, it is safe to assume that they are not as confident about their own parenting as they wish to be. On rare occasions, this won't be the case, but it will be true so often that it should be every educator's bedrock assumption, even with aggressively critical parents. Sometimes, these parents are attributing to the school an issue that actually has roots at home, as we'll explore in the next chapter.

But no matter what the teacher imagines about the home backstory, the educators' mantra about parent communication should begin: *sincere and anxious*.

Assumption 2: Problems are inevitable and often valuable.

This assumption can be hard for teachers to embrace because defensiveness typically kicks in so quickly. Many problems stem from the built-in tensions in the parent-teacher relationship *and* virtually guarantee that every year a great many educators will encounter some kind of stress or difficulty with one or more parents. While most of these situations are ultimately workable, more and more of them are complicated and draining. This can make it difficult to see that many problems turn out to be opportunities. Even when a mother's concern is unfounded or greatly exaggerated, talking with her about it represents an opportunity to learn something useful about the context of her child's life and, often, to be helpful to her (and her child).

In this regard, remembering *sincerity and anxiety* makes it easier to tolerate even unpleasant parents and provides a basis for engaging with them in joint problem-solving.

Assumption 3: The educator is the senior partner and can apply with parents the very skills that work with students.

Just as the school as an institution acts as the senior partner vis à vis the parent body as a whole, each individual educator can take the same role vis à vis parents in any particular interaction. A teacher may be younger than the parents she meets with, may not be a parent herself, may earn a fraction of what they earn, may spend her days with kindergartners, and—especially if it's early in her career or the issue about the student seems serious—may feel apprehensive. But the teacher is still the senior partner when it comes to education. She is the specialist in child development and schooling. She is dealing with parents who (with extremely rare exceptions) are not as savvy about child development as she is and who themselves are anxious.

Holding onto this perspective is a key link to translating the first two assumptions into action. It invites the teacher to employ with parents the skills she employs with students. This may seem counterintuitive. But as the rest of this chapter will illustrate, when in doubt about how to respond to, or how to raise an issue with, a parent, an excellent starting point is to ask oneself, "What would I do if this were a student?" When dealing with students, good educators, like good parents, are caring but clear, friendly but firm, supportive but not enabling. Above all, they listen well and talk straight.

If educators can stay true to these three ways of thinking about the parent-teacher relationship, they will approach parents with much more confidence. Next, here are skills that all teachers will find useful in their toolbox.

FIVE SKILLS EVERY TEACHER NEEDS

Skill 1: Active listening.

Effective communication with parents begins with listening actively. It's vital for gaining information, for conveying interest and empathy, and for building and sustaining cooperation. And the principles of active listening lead naturally into the principles of straight talking when it is the educator's turn to speak.

Active listening has its roots in psychotherapy. It consists of paying close attention to what individuals tell you and to their feelings about what they're telling you, and checking and clarifying to be sure that you've understood both of these things by restating what you've heard. The checking and clarifying allow you to know that you are on the right empathic track. This kind of active listening helps avoid misunderstandings, inclines people to open up and to say more than they otherwise might, and reduces the potential for conflict.

Listening actively invites parents to share their thoughts, questions, or concerns; encourages them to enlarge upon these with examples; and periodically restates the key points they make, testing to be sure the educator has understood correctly. Thus, in a conference, a teacher might ask parents what they see in their child at home, whether they have any questions about the student at school, and so on.

If parents voice a concern ("We've always been told that our daughter is gifted, and she studies hard, but she never gets an A in your class"), the teacher doesn't immediately defend or explain. Instead, the teacher invites the parents to elaborate ("Tell me more about that"), focuses on the student's behavior ("When you say she's working very hard, can you tell me what you mean?"), and—crucially—tries to *understand the meaning of the problem to the parents* ("What is it about this that most concerns you?").

As the picture emerges, the teacher tries to summarize the parents' issue. It may be that they think the teacher is unfair ("It sounds like you really think I'm not giving her the marks she deserves") or that their daughter isn't really gifted, after all ("This has left you wondering whether she's as bright as you've been told") or that their daughter is driven and grade-conscious and might become depressed ("So you're concerned that her reaction could develop into a real psychological problem").

It is important to remember that, in clarifying parents' concerns, the teacher is not *telling* parents what they think or feel but *asking* them, trying out a summary to see whether it captures how they see things. These kinds of responses are the very ones the teacher would make to the student herself if the student came to complain about the grades she received.

A key aspect of active listening is to avoid taking literally any emotionally laden communication, whether it is a loaded question, a small complaint, or a full blast. Whenever parents raise any issue or use any tone that is surprising, challenging, or upsetting, it is ideal, though sometimes difficult, to avoid becoming defensive. Faced with a hostile challenge, teachers typically race to defend themselves, to explain their grading policy, their curriculum, and so on. This can invite further attack. The wise course is to resist the urge to respond without first understanding what stimulated the comment or accusation. Once this is understood, answering is much easier, the potential for conflict is reduced, and the conversation is more likely to stay focused on the student's needs.

Here's an example told by a second grade teacher:

> There was an urgent request from Betsy's mother to call at once. When I reached her, she immediately demanded, in an accusatory voice, "Why are you teaching Egypt that way?" Like she was a prosecutor. My heart sank. "Oh my God," I thought. "She's an Egyptologist. She knows much more about Egypt than I do. She thinks I'm incompetent." I was petrified. As it turned out, she knew nothing about teaching Egypt. In the carpool on the way home Betsy had said something about not remembering the names of the pharaohs. Her mother just wanted me to make sure Betsy wasn't missing anything. I never would have known this if I hadn't screwed my courage up and asked her to tell me about her concern.

For educators, the best response is to be interested and curious—to say to the parent, as this teacher did (and as one would to a student), some version of "tell me more."

There are two reasons why many teachers are hesitant to ask questions of parents, especially when it comes to inviting parents to elaborate on criticisms.

In this context, at a professional development meeting, a teacher once drew laughter and applause from his colleagues by asking, "If somebody starts killing me, why should I try to help them?" This may indeed seem suicidal, until you get used to doing it. It takes a little practice, to be sure, but it is a wonderful way of defusing conflict. Imagine a parent who has said something disparaging or found fault, explicitly or implicitly, with a teacher or administrator. The educator naturally feels an impulse toward self-defense. Without consciously planning it, the parent very likely anticipates this and is ready to intensify the criticism. If the educator, instead of resisting, asks to learn more, this takes some of the wind out of the parent's sails and shows a calm confidence and a genuine interest that are disarming.

The second hesitation grows out of the fear that active listening may imply to parents that a teacher agrees with their diagnosis or desire when this is not the case. Not so. Listening does *not* mean agreeing. It means being sure one has understood the other person's point of view. A teacher who has listened in this way is free to be equally clear. In fact, it is vital to do so.

Skill 2: Asking questions, especially about parental hopes and fears.

Teachers spend their days asking questions—hundreds of them—of students; they are completely comfortable doing so. But many do not feel comfortable asking questions of adults. They may feel that they lack a mandate to question adults, or that they risk being intrusive, or that perhaps the administration will not support a teacher who is seen as intruding. So, what do teachers do instead? They do what comes naturally: They explain and teach and reassure and teach some more.

But asking is more effective because the more questions a teacher asks, the more likely it is that the teacher is going to be able to solve the problem that is bedeviling the parent. Please note, we aren't referring to the *child's* problem. Commonly, the problem is less about the child and more about the parent's struggle with some aspect of the child's development that the parent needs to talk about. In our experience, it takes practice for teachers to be able to ask parents three, four, or more questions. It is a skill well worth practicing.

The two most important questions that educators should ask parents are related to the twin issues of parents' hopes and fears. At the most extreme end, this can involve parents' most cherished dreams and worst nightmares. At the more relaxed end, it can simply mean what parents were imagining and what they now find disappointing. It is almost always possible to get to the bottom of parents' concerns by asking the "hopes and fears" questions and sometimes re-asking them in different ways:

"What were you hoping for?" "What were you wishing would happen?" "What part in the play had you been picturing she would get?"

Questions about dreams should be followed by inquiry about fears:

"What are you worried about for her?" "If she doesn't get into college X, what are you afraid will happen to her?" And then a key follow-up question: "Is she as worried about this as you are?"

The answer to that last question is often "No, and we don't understand why." An answer like that from a parent opens the door to insights that a teacher can provide.

In our experience, the most powerful flashlight in the toolkit is the "hopes and fears" questions, asked with a tone of genuine inquiry. (There is no place for irony or sarcasm here.) Nothing illuminates parents' motivations and perspective more clearly than asking about their hopes and fears.

Skill 3: Claiming the child.

All parents want their children to be known and loved by the school. This is especially true when parents choose an independent school, which is typically smaller than a public school, with smaller class sizes and hence more chance for educators to connect with individual students. It isn't possible for educators to love all students (not all students are lovable all the time!), but it is vital for educators to let the parents know that the teachers know their child as a learner. To do this is to go beyond the standard opening of many teacher-parent conferences: the recitation of nice things about a student ("She is a wonderful artist," "He is a wonderful friend to his friends," and so on).

We are not criticizing a strengths-based approach to describing students; noting strengths is never a mistake. But it is not sufficient. The teacher needs to describe an interaction with the child that puts her into the picture. Contrast "She's a very good artist" with this: "I was watching her paint last week, and she uses an extraordinary array of colors." Here the teacher has put herself in the picture; she has described being with the child, watching the child, appreciating the child. That's a huge difference to a parent's ear. The parent thinks, "The teacher was *right there, appreciating my child.*"

What can an educator say if the child is not as gifted or if the teacher has not cemented a good relationship with the student? What to say, for example, about an indifferent 10th grade history student? The default educator observation is often generic: "He could be working harder. He has the ability; I'm hoping he makes more of an effort next semester." A parent learns little from this.

Contrast this with something more specific: "I have been trying to connect with your son in history. I don't think he likes the course. Has he enjoyed history or social studies in the past?" This is authentic, and it also puts the teacher in the picture. The teacher is in there trying to forge a relationship with the indifferent learner.

Claiming a child may be the first step in creating an alliance with a parent that can bear some weight. Parents are willing to accept insights from an educator who is clearly interested in being close to their child and invested in his or her learning. In a 13-year journey through school, there are always some hard things that parents are going to need to hear. Claiming a child provides the foundation for a bridge between educator and parent, a bridge that can support the weight of straight talk when it is needed.

Skill 4: Straight talking.

For most educators, the primary concern in dealing with parents is how to deliver bad news, especially if the parent is not a good listener. The key is to be simple and direct and, when the news is bad, candid and concerned. Several techniques can help with this.

- **Follow the Rule of Three.** Simplicity and directness begin with the Rule of Three. In a conference where a child's problems are discussed, parents are unlikely to remember more than three points clearly. In all but a few cases, they are already feeling enough stress to impair their concentration and memory. This puts a premium on organizing the message and using topic sentences, which don't always come naturally to educators. Some of the most gifted teachers are not adept at summarizing a student's performance succinctly. Many—especially elementary faculty who still teach in true developmental, child-centered ways—are inclined to discuss their curriculum and a student's progress in an eclectic style that digresses, repeats, leaps ahead, circles back, and so on.

  Parents today need a more structured, focused presentation. This might begin, "I have three key things I want to emphasize about Jane: She's a very hard worker, she's doing well in most subjects, but she is having some trouble with math." The teacher can then follow up with data and examples for each of the three points.

  As straightforward as this approach may sound, it is not common, especially when the problem area is a touchy one. Teachers like to start with the positive news about a student before turning to the negative because this sets a better tone for the discussion. (It also postpones the possibility of—and reduces the time for—parental upsets.) Beginning with a student's strengths surely makes good sense, but it generally works best to include the bad news headline in the topic sentence. This gives the parents a framework for what they're going to hear, and it also provides a kind of upfront reminder to them and the teacher that there is an area of concern that needs to be addressed.

- **Avoid fudging the issue, and instead frame it in clear, concrete terms.** One of the most common ways that teacher-parent communication goes awry is when teachers have unwelcome news to present, are afraid of doing so, and try to minimize or sugarcoat the data. Too often, they put the problem topic last on the agenda and fudge it. They are not concrete enough, resorting to generalizations that, they hope, will convey their concern without provoking distress or attack.

    Unfortunately, this not only fails to inform parents accurately, but it can also leave them doubting the teacher's connection to their child, which only increases the likelihood of upsetting them. As we noted above, all parents want to know that their child's teacher knows their child. If they doubt this, they are likely to doubt what the teacher tells them about the child, and rightly so. Confidence, like God and the devil, is in the details: A teacher confirms that she or he knows a student by being specific. And the key to being specific is to frame the issue instead of fudging it. Framing the issue means to first precede it with something that confirms the educator's authentic concern and caring and to then present the straight summary.

    The process begins with thinking through what to say, in the bluntest terms, no punches pulled, if the teacher dared. "He isn't misbehaving because he's gifted and getting bored. He's terrified of making mistakes." Or "She keeps mocking another girl, sometimes in very cruel ways."

    The goal is then to say as much of this as possible, softened as little as possible and preceded by something that will make it hearable. Thus: "I know that you see him as gifted and bored by the pace of the class, but I see something very different. He seems terribly afraid of getting anything wrong. Whenever he does, he grimaces, and that's when he starts acting out." Or "I have a real concern that I hope we can think about together: She's been consistently teasing and making fun of one of the other girls, sometimes in ways that have left that girl in tears."

Effective framing often begins with phrases such as "I'm concerned that…" or "I'm worried that…." Sometimes it begins "I'm puzzled that…." It can even begin "I'm not sure I can say this just right, so please hear me out. I'll do the best I can and then I'll be eager to hear your thoughts." After this, the teacher can almost always say the blunt sentence straight out.

- **Remember that tone of voice matters enormously.** Needless to say, none of these suggestions will work if delivered as a glib verbal formula. The teacher's tone must confirm sincere concern and caring for the student and a desire to help things work better. At times, it needs to contain a measure of firmness, sometimes even of warning.

- **Maintain resolve.** Again, these suggestions won't work if the teacher immediately backs down in the face of challenge. If the parents of the boy above ask, "Are you saying he's not gifted?" the response needs to be something like "He seems perfectly capable, but his work in my class doesn't give me evidence that he's gifted, and in any case, his misbehavior always occurs after he's made a mistake." If the parents of the girl ask, "Are you saying she's cruel to this other student?" the response has to be "Yes, unfortunately, I am."

Directness in such situations can be followed by "I hope we can think together about how to help your child with this." Often, there is something the school can do to foster a positive change. But teachers (and administrators) should not hold back when they see a need for parents to take action at home. Being clear, descriptive, specific, and concrete requires courage. But it projects a teacher's authority, compels parents' attention, and confirms that the teacher knows the student. These are all crucial to building collaboration.

Skill 5: Shaping the collaboration by running a crisp, professional meeting.

Many educators fail to plan their meetings with parents or think through what they are hoping to achieve. Just letting a meeting happen is a mistake. Teachers cannot always give a child an A, but they can run a professional meeting, and in that way they will have an impact on parents. Educators need to think about the goals of the meeting and imagine themselves managing the time and the flow of the conversation. The following steps will help:

- **Start clearly.** Typically, parent-teacher conferences are relatively short, often less than a half-hour. They occur on the teacher's turf, and the teacher should structure them by setting an agenda. The teacher can say, "We only have 20 minutes. I'm eager to hear what you might want to tell or ask me, and I have three things I want to be sure to go over with you."

- **End clearly.** A great many teachers (and not a few administrators) admit that they have a hard time ending meetings with parents. What's needed is to keep an eye on the clock and be ready to deliver a five-minute warning ("We only have five minutes left, and I still have one key item to cover").

  Then, at the close of the conference, it is ideal to restate the key themes that have been addressed, both those brought up by parents and those presented by the teacher. It is also important to underscore areas where teacher and parents have different views or outright disagreements and what, if anything, has been adopted as a next step in addressing these.

  When an issue is especially serious, the meeting will often occur in an administrator's office. In such cases, shaping these discussions is especially important, and many of the techniques for staying on track are the same. Whoever leads the meeting should begin by stating its purpose and noting its time frame. If time is running out and there is clearly much more to discuss, it is often wiser to arrange another session rather than extend the current one, especially if the educators involved are on a tight schedule. Among other things, this sends a tacit message that educators' time is important, which can help everyone stay on topic in future meetings. Although it may not seem so, this is also a way of forming an effective collaboration with parents because it provides role clarity and establishes boundaries, which in turn enables everyone to relax a bit and feel more confident that they know what to expect.

As we've said, the five essential skills outlined here are effective for managing relationships with parents. Variations on these skills can also be useful when parents try to get their concerns addressed outside of regular channels through end runs and ambushes.

These days, many more parents threaten to go over the teacher's head to raise their concern or get their way. For the teacher, the only useful response to such a threat is to be direct and invite the parent to go right ahead—and to immediately alert the appropriate administrator. As for parents who go straight to the top without trying to raise their concern with the teacher, a good administrator or head of school will almost always insist that the parents have the full conversation with the teacher first. If the issue still remains, the administrator will actively consult with and include the teacher in the response to the parents.

It is also much more common now for parents to want instant responses to their concerns and to "ambush" teachers about questions and concerns, large and small. This can happen in the parking lot, on the soccer sidelines, at the supermarket, even on the phone or through texts at home in the evening. Teachers find all this intrusive, yet they don't want to seem rude or withholding. So they take the call or answer the text, stay on it too long, and resent it.

In such situations, it is once again important for teachers to value their own time. Every teacher should set a clear limit: "I only have five minutes." It is almost always best to suggest and, if need be, to insist, politely but firmly, on a conference or a call at school. This means saying, "I'd love to talk with you about this, so please contact me to set up a time to meet" or "I'd be very happy to discuss this with you but I can't do it now. Let's plan a time to talk at school." Teachers can find this easier to do if the school has published guidelines to this effect. And here, again, teachers will rarely go wrong by being the senior partner, by keeping in mind, "What would I say or do if this were a student?"

We hope that all of the foregoing has made clear that these perspectives are not ploys, nor is this basic toolkit a set of maneuvers to use *against* parents.

Instead, these techniques are a way to *engage with* parents constructively in the service of their children. This always involves listening carefully, it often demands speaking directly, and it sometimes requires setting limits. But the goal is always to act in the interest of giving students the best possible chance to flourish.

BEYOND THE BASIC TOOLKIT

At the outset of this chapter, we said that the methods in this basic toolkit, though simple, are not always easy. Fortunately, most parents, as we've emphasized, aren't adversarial. Even if they overreact in their distress about an issue, most, at heart, want to be good participants in the school community.

But not all. So sometimes the basic toolkit isn't enough. Active listening, inquiring about hopes and fears, claiming the child, using straight talk, and running a good meeting will clear up confusion, lead to insight, and resolve conflict most of the time. But not always. The parents we call the 5 percenters present special challenges that require special measures. Dealing successfully with them requires an advanced toolkit. We open that next.

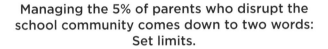

Managing the 5% of parents who disrupt the
school community comes down to two words:
Set limits.

Chapter 10

The Advanced Toolkit

The 5 percenters—parents who are clinically anxious and incompetent, unresponsive, or intimidating—all make educators feel frustrated and dismayed. In the case of intimidators, they can inspire fear as well. The basic toolkit in the previous chapter is insufficient to deal with these individuals for two reasons.

First, the challenges that 5 percenters present involve boundary-breaking—that is, asking or demanding, often repeatedly, that the school make significant exceptions to its practices or policies and often doing so in a way that violates the school's basic norms and values.

Second, whether because of personality, cognitive style, or other factors, 5 percenters can't be reasoned with.

This book's basic toolkit is designed to help educators connect with parents who are fundamentally positive and to do so in ways that will help the parents reflect on their hopes and fears, a process in which they often come to realize something important about themselves and their relationship to their child and the school. The basic toolkit assumes that insight will lead to behavior change and, specifically, to an improved, more collaborative connection with the school. It can work only if the parents are amenable to insight, if they have some self-reflective capacity. Five percenters do not.

As Chapter 5 noted, a small number of parents don't warrant the presumption of good mental health that schools tend to grant everyone. These parents suffer from mental illness, including personality disorders. This means that they may be high-functioning in some respects (their careers, say), but in other areas of life, they consistently distort reality. They may have a misguided view of their children and a deep mistrust of institutions, including the school. A few of these parents are truly narcissistic (more on this below).

The goal of the advanced toolkit can be summarized in just two words: *setting limits*.

By this we mean asserting the school's values and policies, naming the violation of these that a parent is committing, and announcing the school's nonnegotiable decision about how the matter will be resolved. Unlike the basic toolkit, the advanced toolkit is not about promoting insight and self-reflection; it is about insisting on immediate behavior change. It calls for meetings and conversations that are short and sometimes blunt. It calls for facing up directly to conflict with parents—and for addressing their weaknesses. And it calls for not accommodating parents who threaten—and some who plead with—the school.

We've referred here to "the school" and not to "the teacher" for a reason. Setting limits on parents is above a teacher's pay grade; it must almost always be done by an administrator. With rare exceptions, teachers lack the power and status to set limits on parents. A teacher, no matter how experienced, can only use an *I* voice (*my* classroom, *my* curriculum). An administrator speaks with a more powerful *we* voice in the name of the institution (*our* policy, the way *we* do things here). It's a vital difference. A teacher may quite accurately say, "What you're asking for is against our school policy," but the impact of the sentence is much stronger when an administrator is the one who says it. Whenever a teacher encounters a real 5 percenter, it's typically best to hand the situation on to an administrator straight away.

We'll start with the least threatening of the 5 percenters, the parents who are anxious and incompetent and those who are unresponsive. Then we'll concentrate on the ones who are the most challenging, the intimidators.

Before we do, a special note. In what follows, some of the language we suggest, printed on a page, may sound cold. So we want to stress that tone matters hugely with 5 percenters. Since the goal is behavior change, not insight, the ideal tone, while never disrespectful, doesn't radiate warmth and an open invitation for parents to express themselves at length. It combines inquiry and genuine concern with a sober, this-is-serious inflection. In the most difficult cases, it is flat and matter-of-fact, a directive.

THE ANXIOUS AND INCOMPETENT

Clinically anxious parents (overwhelmingly, though not exclusively, mothers) and those who present as incompetent ask for special assistance from teachers, coaches, and advisers, both for themselves and on behalf of their child. Educators who comply soon find that one request leads to another and that they are endlessly playing whack-a-mole, resolving one parental issue only to be presented with another. Here are two examples.

Mrs. Brown, the mother of Julie, a first grader, called the teacher urgently. She had arranged a playdate for Julie with a classmate, Christine, but Christine's mother had just cancelled, saying that Christine didn't want to play with Julie. Would the teacher please tell Julie that the playdate was off? When the teacher asked, "Wouldn't it be better if you told her?" Mrs. Brown began to weep, saying, "Oh, it will be so hard for her, I can't bear it. Can't you please do it?" Reluctantly, the teacher agreed. This turned out to be the first of multiple requests for her to essentially co-parent Julie, to deliver messages to her that Mrs. Brown was afraid to deliver, and to intervene on Julie's behalf with other students and parents.

Another parent, Mrs. Green, arranged a neuropsychological evaluation over the summer for her son, Tim, that revealed some mild learning differences, which she then used as the occasion to contact the school daily. She took turns calling individual teachers, the adviser, the learning specialist, coaches, even the athletic director, always with a concern about Tim or a request for special consideration. In February, when the educators finally met to discuss the case, they realized that she had already contacted school personnel nearly 500 times.

Neither Mrs. Brown nor Mrs. Green was unpleasant or impolite. Both were obviously worried, and Mrs. Brown seemed truly helpless. In each case, the teachers and others who dealt with the mother started out feeling kindly disposed and eager to help; then began to be concerned about the impact on the student of the exaggerated concern; and ultimately found dealing with the mother a frustrating, intrusive, time-consuming burden. Without being discourteous, both parents were, in effect, being disrespectful, imposing repeatedly on the educators with inappropriate and excessive requests.

The basic message parents like this need to hear is a kind but firm no. There needs to be a clear stop to their requests, not only because the requests impose on the teacher but also because accommodating them makes the teacher complicit in the parents' misdiagnosis of their children's fragility.

The message to both parents should include a direct naming of the problematic behavior. For Mrs. Brown, this would be "The things you're asking are things a parent needs to do." If a teacher were to say this and it were to cause Mrs. Brown distress, she would need to be handed on to a division head, who could have a further conversation with her to explore her fears about Julie and, conceivably, to refer her for parent guidance counseling.

For Mrs. Green, the February discovery would lead immediately to the division head arranging a meeting with her where the heart of the message would be "You've contacted us nearly 500 times since September, and we can't have this continue. Also, you keep voicing concerns about problems with your son that we don't see, and we need to understand why."

THE UNRESPONSIVE

For most 5 percenter parents, setting limits means making them stop. But this is not the case for the unresponsive, those who ignore the school's concerns or fail to follow through on its recommendations for a student. The unresponsives need to be mobilized on their child's behalf. For them, setting limits means making them start, as in this example.

Jay, now a fourth grader, had been admitted to the school in second grade despite some worrisome signs. He was soon flagged as having significant problems. He couldn't stay on task, seemed unmotivated, and was often aggressive with other students. Each year's teacher had described all this to his parents, who seemed only mildly troubled. The school had initially recommended a screening by its lower school counselor, but the parents thought Jay would grow out of his difficulties. The school relented. In third grade, the teacher recommended a full outside psychological evaluation. The parents said they would look into it, but they did nothing. The school didn't insist. By fourth grade, Jay had fallen well behind his peers and was a constant behavioral problem in the class, occupying a disproportionate amount of the teacher's time and energy.

With parents like Jay's, a school doesn't have six meetings—it has the same meeting six times. By the middle of fourth grade, his teachers were truly alarmed and laid out their concerns in full to their division head. She summoned Jay's parents to an urgent meeting. Her message at the meeting was simple and direct:

> We are extremely concerned about Jay. Extremely. We don't understand why you don't respond to our concerns or follow through on our recommendations. We wonder whether you don't believe us or whether you think we don't know what we're doing—and if so, why you keep him at our school.

When Jay's parents said they were still considering an evaluation but were uncertain whether it was really necessary, the division head told them, "We want to help Jay flourish, but we can't do that without a full evaluation. We need this before spring break, or we won't be able to welcome him back next year."

THE INTIMIDATORS

These are the hardest parents for a school to deal with. Mostly, though not exclusively, fathers, they are essentially bullies. They make no bones about what they want. They demand that rules be waived, exceptions made, policies upended, teachers and coaches they dislike fired. And it's not just that they make inappropriate demands. They are disrespectful, rude, often engage in personal attacks on teachers and administrators, and demean and threaten them. They repeatedly violate the school's policies, values, and norms of conduct.

Some are true narcissists and "externalizers," as psychologists call them. They see every problem they encounter as caused by others' incompetence or malevolence. No matter how intelligent they may be, they demonstrate arrested social-emotional development. In this they resemble undisciplined adolescents, and a school will rarely go wrong by treating them as such.

But easier said than done.

Unlike the anxious/incompetent and the unresponsive parents, intimidators inspire fear. If a father calls a teacher and starts out, "You gave our son a B and you need to change it to an A!" it's likely to trigger immediate apprehension. We've already made the case that educators are classic conflict avoiders. This is less true of administrators than of teachers, but the trait is ubiquitous in schools. Too often, educators at all levels vacillate between placating intimidators and reasoning with them, trying anything to avoid confronting them, and hoping that somehow they'll see the light. Over and over, we hear about schools enduring months, even years, of gross misbehavior by a parent before administrators recognize that they are dealing with serious psychopathology that won't yield to normal intervention and requires firm limits.

Although all 5 percenters are hard for administrators to handle, this is especially true for intimidators. When a parent begins a conversation by ordering a teacher to change a student's grade, it's naïve to assume that he can be talked out of it. What's *not* likely to be helpful is for the teacher to try to explain her grading policy or convince the father that the son's grade is justified. It's best for her to acknowledge the discomfort the request causes her, invoke school policy, and signal that administrative reinforcements will be arriving.

All this requires only three sentences: "I understand that you're unhappy about the grade, but your request makes me quite uncomfortable. School policy doesn't permit changing a grade at a parent's request. However, I will certainly convey your request to the head of the middle school."

If a teacher's encounter with an intimidator is scary enough, she may enlist an administrator for a follow-up with the parent or for the next regularly scheduled conference. If so, the teacher and administrator involved should prep together in advance, so that they understand their goals and roles for the meeting. (It's remarkable how often independent school educators will go into difficult meetings armed only with their goodwill, not with a plan or a designated goal.)

When a situation does reach a dean, a division head, or the head of school, the administrator usually has to address not just the parent's boundary-breaking demand (change the grade, fire the coach) but also his boundary-breaking approach (demeaning a teacher, screaming at a coach). Dan Vorenberg, head at Mirman School (CA), tells these parents:

> You have a message about your child that you want us to address. But it's like you taped it to a rock and threw it through our window. You want us just to respond to what you wrote, but we can't because we have a rock and broken glass all over the place.

Another head gives a similar message: "We have two issues here: your concern, which we want to address, and the way you're expressing it, which makes that impossible. If you want us to take your issue seriously, you can't yell and swear at us."

Swearing is very rare, yelling, less so. But the more egregious the intimidator's behavior—the more it violates the school's basic norms and values or the more publicly it does so—the sooner it needs an administrative response and the higher up the leadership ladder that responder must be.

At the very start of the 2020 coronavirus pandemic that caused schools to close and begin teaching online, a father at a small religious school decided that he would not submit his reenrollment deposit for the following year until he saw how well the faculty managed the new distance learning. He informed the school of this *after* he had circulated an online petition about his plan and convinced 100 parents to sign it—a catastrophic threat to the school. That father's concern, at heart, was not totally unreasonable. But whenever a parent goes public like this, he becomes an adversary of his child's school. Surprisingly, many parents who go public don't grasp this because they see their relationship to the school as transactional—money paid for service rendered—and as amenable to the exercise of their personal influence and power. Running a campaign against the school or against a particular teacher or coach seems to them a legitimate way to advance their own interests. In such situations, the head of school needs to meet with the parent and explain how the public attack has affected teachers, students, and coaches—even the parent's own child, which sometimes happens. Quite often, the parent has no idea how far-reaching and upsetting his campaign has been.

Here's an example from a public high school. The mother of a freshman, intensely focused on the idea that he was truly gifted and must eventually be admitted to Harvard, began barraging all five of his teachers with long, hostile emails, accusing them of not knowing what they were doing, not being rigorous enough, and not caring about her son. No matter how the teachers responded, she remained intractable. So they printed her emails and took them to the school's principal.

He telephoned her and said: "We have a serious problem. We love your son, but we don't like you." (How's that for an opening line?) He continued, "You've managed to offend all five of your son's teachers. It will be awful if, for his four years here, despite how much we already love him, no one wants to teach him because of you."

The mother had no idea how offensive her behavior had been. The principal concluded by saying, "You and I need to find a way to reboot your relationship with your son's teachers—so that he can have a great four years here."

For a very few parents, their campaign against some aspect of the school can become all-consuming, a raison d'être. There are complex psychological reasons for this, but understanding the reasons is not likely to lead to a resolution. There is only one way to stop such parents, and that is via an ultimatum: They must end their campaign or the family will not be offered a contract for their children to return next year.

The grandiose father of an 11th-grade girl who was the best female volleyball player in the state was utterly wrapped up in his daughter's career. He acted as though her talent gave him license to second-guess her coach publicly. He bombarded the athletic department with harshly critical emails. The coach had taken the team to the state finals for the past two years, but the team had lost—and the losses were unbearable for the father. He began to campaign for the coach's removal. He gave dinner parties for team members and their parents where he lobbied the players and urged them to refuse to attend their traditional end-of-season reviews with the coach.

Multiple phone calls and meetings with school personnel failed to dissuade him. It was a long, grueling war that ended only when the athletic director called the father in and asked if the administration could help him find a new school for his daughter. When he replied that his daughter really wanted to stay, the athletic director imposed severe limitations on his involvement with the team for her senior year, any violation of which would mean that his daughter would not be allowed to play. That, and only that, changed the father's behavior.

Intimidators can be hardest to deal with when they're not entirely in the wrong, such as when their misconduct occurs in response to a teacher error. Teachers are human; they sometimes make bad mistakes. Troubled parents can become obsessed with a need for restitution, as in the case of Edward, a sullen, entitled seventh grader, who disliked his science teacher. One day, when the teacher was introducing a lab assignment, Edward grumbled his disapproval. Irritated, the teacher, his voice full of sarcasm, said to the class, "Wait, everyone. We can't do anything until we hear from Prince Edward."

When Edward related this to his parents, they erupted. They called the head of school and demanded the teacher's immediate termination. The head eventually required the teacher to apologize to Edward and his parents—sarcasm toward students has no place in the classroom. But this was not enough for the family. They wrote several letters insisting that the teacher be terminated or at least required to apologize publicly at an assembly. They even drafted the text they wanted him to read there and faxed it to the school, where it was seen by staff and publicly discussed. They gave up only when the head finally told them that the issue was closed and that if they wanted to pursue it, they should contact the school's lawyer.

WHEN PUSH COMES TO SHOVE

You can't win 'em all. When every remedy has been exhausted, sometimes the only true solution is excommunication. It's a step schools take rarely and never easily. Everyone feels saddened by the failure to find a workable solution. But the health of the school community and the protection of the faculty can require expelling an intimidator family or occasionally an unresponsive family, even when the students involved are quite wonderful and completely innocent. In addition to educators' strong propensity to avoid open conflict, their reluctance to have children suffer for their parents' conduct is another reason that schools so often put up with outrageous behavior for so long. But there is invariably palpable relief among faculty and staff when the head of school decides to end the drama.

In some schools where enrollment is problematic, excluding a family poses a financial challenge: lost tuition. This is an understandable concern, although the failure to expel a true boundary-breaking family can actually increase the risk of losing other families who don't want to put up with the excessive misbehavior. If a school doesn't want to move to immediate expulsion, it can at least make it much harder for a parent to misbehave. It can set clear, strong restrictions on the parent, as with the volleyball father above. Depending on the case, these restrictions can include actions such as the following:

- Confining the parent's communication to one specific administrator and clarifying that no faculty member will respond to the parent's emails and calls

- Sharply limiting the number of messages that will be acknowledged

- Seeking a restraining order to control—even eliminate—a parent's access to the school and its people

These conditions should be presented—briefly, directly, and in person—as decisions, not as items for discussion, and followed up in a formal letter.

IT'S BUSINESS, NOT PERSONAL

This chapter, with its focus on setting limits, might be seen as being about how to get tough with tough parents. We know that suggesting that educators confront difficult parents head-on is a big ask. As we've said here and previously in this book, getting tough with other adults is not one of educators' strengths. School people are helpers, caregivers, nurturers, mentors, guides. They prefer the daily company of young children and adolescents and thrive on their engagement with students. Their work is personal, not business. This distinction, famously, comes from the classic film *The Godfather*. The movie turns on a series of gangland assassinations, which, as three of the characters say, aren't personal— they're just business.

In school, *everything* is personal, which is exactly how we all want it. But precisely because educators take their work so personally, they are particularly vulnerable to criticism. Their skin is thin, not thick.

It's unrealistic to expect teachers and administrators to shrug conflict off, to not feel scared, hurt, or defensive when an intimidator gives them a blast of withering criticism. But as psychologists, we know that although people can't stop an initial feeling, they can learn to manage it.

For example, they can develop a signal to say to themselves that helps them control their initial reaction and be less flummoxed. Any signal helps. One signal could be "It's not *personal*." This is important because, even though intimidators often insult people in very personal terms ("You don't care about my son!" "You're a terrible coach!"), most of their attacks are not truly personal in that they're not reserved for a specific person. These parents would treat *any* teacher or coach who disappoints them in the very same way.

Another signal could be "Whatever we did, we did nothing to make this person as crazy as [he or she] sounds at this moment."

Because anxious and helpless parents, unresponsive parents, and intimidator parents can consume so much time and energy and cause such distress, the signal can also be a reminder of three important facts.

They are only 5% of the parent body.

The goal is to change their behavior, not to make them see the light.

The key is to set limits, just as it is with misbehaving children.

■

Five practical tasks can help senior administrators help teachers—and save everyone time and agony.

Chapter 11

A Guide for Administrators on Training and Supporting Teachers

This chapter is directed largely to school administrators, especially division directors and heads of school, and we start it by apologizing. We want to give you some ideas about how to train teachers to be more effective in working with parents. We're hoping that the book you've just read (unless you've skipped to this chapter) has provided some helpful thoughts in that area. We're also hoping to help you craft policies that will shape the parent-teacher relationship and the parent-school partnership so that it works better for everyone. But we know that the last thing you may feel you need is something else to do.

We have worked with and respected school administrators for decades. We think we understand a lot about what the jobs require, and we know very well that it's always a very long list: more visiting classes, more supervision feedback to teachers, better curricula, more innovation, more communication with parents, better professional development workshops. In other words: more, more, better, better, and more. It often feels as if there is no end to it.

Our defense for imposing further is this: We believe that by restructuring the parent-school partnership and improving the parent-teacher relationship, administrators and heads of school will save themselves time and agony down the line. What we are seeing in the schools we have visited is that parents are taking up increasing amounts of attention. Happily, much of it still goes to teachers and students, but there is no question that parents have been demanding a larger share of that most precious resource, time. Independent schools must be responsive to their customers, but they also have to protect the integrity of the enterprise. Here are ways to do that.

FIVE TASKS TO HELP WITH TRAINING AND SUPPORT

Task 1: Review school policies regarding parents—and don't invite the camel into the tent.

We have taken the position that educators should be the senior partners in the home-school partnership. Even though parents know their children best, when it comes to schooling, educators know what's best for students. It's important, therefore, that schools craft policies that reflect this reality. Most schools' viewbooks and handbooks suggest a vague and joyous—and equal—partnership. As one handbook reads: "We are partners in supporting the growth and development of your child." Of course, but what, exactly, does that mean?

Years ago, we consulted to a school that had started as a small, under-resourced parent co-op where moms and dads were required to volunteer in the classroom weekly. As the school grew from a tiny co-op to a K-8 school of more than 400 students, all of those parent co-op practices fell away. They were never scheduled, rarely mentioned, never enforced. But 25 years after the school's founding, when the head tried to change its bylaws, a ferocious minority of parents mobilized to keep the original bylaws because they didn't want to lose their "rights." Having observed parents suggesting curricular changes (such as Singapore math), attacking disciplinary policies, trying to get their children waived out of requirements, and attempting to build coalitions to dictate the hiring and firing of teachers, we think it's unwise to encourage parents into a partnership that is unspecified. Indeed, we find that many schools are unwittingly inviting the camel's nose under the tent.

Therefore, every administrative team needs to take the time to review the school's policy on parent-teacher relationships and see what is addressed and what is left unaddressed. Does the policy describe only an idealized relationship, or does it contain specifics? Does it provide guidance on steps parents should take regarding contacting teachers and administrators? Does it contain guidance about when—and when not—to call or text teachers? Does it have any language about limits?

One way that an administrative team could approach this task would be to go back and find some of the most successful cases of school-parent conflict resolution in the last few years, and also some of the worst. Then the team could ask:

> What did we do right, and what did we do wrong? Where did we set limits, and where did we fail to set limits? What did the teachers involved not anticipate, and what did they not say? Would a change to our policy have been helpful to them or to us? Would it have guided our efforts or given us something helpful to say to parents?

This kind of review is tough to do because the well-resolved cases simply evaporate as they are assimilated into the daily life of the school, while the painful cases remain as unforgettable psychological scars. But the soul-searching such a review requires is worth the effort to apply lessons from the past and prevent problems in the future.

Another useful step is for the school's leadership to ask faculty what they understand about the school's policies about parent emails, phone calls, and texts; complaints about grades; invitations to dinner; gifts to teachers; and so on. Do the teachers feel that they have adequate guidance? If not, it is important to review these (for example, the kind of email/texting policy we recommended in Chapter 8) and to be very clear about which provisions are mandatory and which are advisory.

Task 2: Remember that first-year teachers need orientation.

Over our years of consulting, we've had a chance to interview many teachers about their first year in an independent school. Whether they're beginners or they're veterans who came from a public or parochial school, they almost universally praise the quality of their colleagues, the experience of collegiality, the autonomy they enjoy, the good behavior and motivation of the students, and the resources available to them.

When asked about any negative or simply "weird" experiences, they almost always cite the parents: their powerful presence as customers, their particular demands, and their intensity.

Administrators should be aware that, not infrequently, first-year teachers are asked challenging or intimidating questions. "Do you have children?" is a classic one that parents ask new, young female teachers. It feels intrusive and can imply doubt about their competence. (We suggest answering this question with a question. If the teacher is not a mother she can reply with an amiable "No, I don't," and then a pleasant—and slightly curious—"Does that worry you?" or "Why do you ask?" If the teacher is a mother she can say yes, but it is still valuable to add "Why do you ask?") Other questions are explicitly or implicitly condescending. For example, parents asked a new Spanish teacher from Mexico who was just starting at a girls' school in New York, "We hear you're from Mexico. How did you get here?" They might simply have been wondering how she had selected that particular school, but she heard it as an inquiry into her immigration status and was immobilized by the question.

It would be helpful to new teachers not just to go over the school's policies but to teach them about the 95 percenters and the 5 percenters, to reassure them that the vast majority of parents are reasonable and workable and often quite lovely. Finally, every young or first-year teacher needs to be encouraged to reach out to administrators sooner rather than later when facing a vexing parent dilemma. We have encountered too many teachers who, perhaps ashamed that they have not wrangled the situation, wait too long before seeking help from administrators. Turning things over to a division director frees a teacher to focus on students, which, after all, is what every teacher really wants to do.

Schools are full of busy people, each involved in hundreds of interactions per day, and time is scarce. There is never enough of it for all the meetings and professional development opportunities that leaders wish to arrange. But providing good upfront orientation about the relationship between independent schools, parents, and teachers can save large amounts of time *and* stress for new teachers—and for their administrators.

Task 3: Provide periodic training to the faculty as a whole.

All teachers benefit from initial formal training on how to manage the parent-teacher relationship and from periodic refreshers, both because of the high and rising level of parent engagement in independent schools and because more of this engagement involves parents-as-anxious-customers.

We recommend that perhaps every four years, the administration should provide a periodic review for the entire faculty. This would include an overview of the fundamentals of the school's guidelines governing communication, complaints about curriculum and teaching, chronic issues like math placement, and, always, disciplinary matters. This might be a time when administrators could go over some memorable (or infamous) parent cases (without naming names) so that everyone could review what went wrong and what went right in the situation.

On an annual basis, it can be helpful for each division of the school to review this book's Chapter 9, the basic toolkit (active listening, asking questions about hopes and fears, claiming the child, straight talking, running a crisp professional meeting). A good time for this is just before parent-teacher conferences—in our experience, even among veteran faculty, anxiety is always heightened at conference time. Once the conferences are over, it's often good to earmark some time at the next faculty meeting for a review of any special issues or challenges that arose, any potentially difficult conversations that went well, and the like.

Task 4: Make more productive use of back-to-school night.

It's always helpful for teachers to get some support before back-to-school night. Speaking from our experience as parents, we usually found these events to be sweet, educational, and a bit uncomfortable.

For one thing, parents are not sure what their role is supposed to be. Are they meant to be fascinated by their child's curriculum? Should they just approve it, or are they allowed to question it? For another, with some exceptions, most teachers seem a bit uncomfortable and defensive in front of a group of parents. They are accustomed to teaching children, not grown-ups, and, as Chapter 1 noted, they're apprehensive about being judged and found wanting. Also, there are always parents who want the teacher to tell them how their child is doing, even though these evenings typically happen very early in the school year and are not supposed to be a time to discuss any particular students. Occasionally, there are a few parents who use the occasion to air complaints about too much homework or some other grievance. Most faculty feel real relief when the evening is over. Happily, most parents leave with a positive impression of their children's teachers.

We wish that back-to-school nights could be put to better use by having teachers address the worries that most parents have. For example, in many schools there is a transition point—from third to fourth grade, say, or from lower to middle school—where the workload ratchets up significantly. This can cause short-term panic among students and upset among their parents. Often, there is a predictable sequence of student and parent distress in the early fall, followed by students adapting to the workload—some quickly, the rest before winter break. Surprisingly, many schools where there is such a pattern don't routinely give parents a heads-up. Back-to-school night is an ideal time to do so.

We know that these evenings need to give parents an overview of the curriculum that will be covered, but it can also be really helpful to parents to anticipate their predictable worries and fears, like the developmental flashpoints addressed in Chapters 2 and 3. It's an opportunity for educators to reassure parents that their children are in good hands by sharing their knowledge of child development (for example, that girl cliques are almost inevitable in seventh grade and that girls survive them). Administrators can remind teachers to include some attention to parents' common developmental worries. Normalizing these worries is never a mistake.

Task 5: Include work with parents as part of a teacher's formal evaluation process.

In our experience, about one-third of independent schools have a well-designed, fully implemented teacher evaluation program; one-third have a mediocre program to which they pay lip service; and one-third do no systematic teacher evaluation at all. The situation is actually better than it was 20 years ago, when a great many schools we visited did no teacher assessment. But it remains a shame that so many schools still do a middling—or worse—job of evaluating faculty because, although teachers generally don't think of it this way, a positive formal evaluation is perhaps the best defense they can have in the face of irrational parental criticism.

If, as we believe, working with parents looms as an ever-larger part of what all educators do, then it is only sensible to make that work part of their formal assessment. When administrators worry about the way a teacher relates to parents, the administrators should step in quickly, before further problems develop, and work with the teacher to improve parent communication. We believe that most teachers can grow in this area, but few schools ask them explicitly to do so.

Effective communication with parents can never be the central feature of a teacher's job, but it can be an area of growth and greater strength. It's also one that can be particularly valuable in schools where enrollment challenges make it vital to retain families.

FINAL NOTES ON THE HEAD OF SCHOOL AND PARENTS

As in all other things, the head of school sets the model for how to think about parents and how to respond to them. If the head is obsessed with enrollment and is willing to promise things and cut special deals with parents in order to put "butts in seats," as one head described it to us, then the faculty knows not to expect protection from difficult parents.

If the head acts like a social worker, meeting endlessly with any anxious parent who needs hand-holding, then the empaths on the faculty will do their best to follow suit, while others will feel disdain.

If the head is seen as someone who expects the best behavior of all adults, including parents, then teachers will feel protected and will be better able to put appropriate limits on parents.

The ideal head of school will, of course, occupy that perfect place by being a whole-hearted advocate for parents and a robust champion of teachers. Parents will experience the head as always interested in them and their children. As one veteran head said to us, "I feel such empathy for parents because their children's development can be so confusing for them."

At the same time, teachers will feel understood and protected because the head stops by their classrooms, appreciates their assemblies, writes notes valuing their work, and really "gets" what their teaching involves. Ordinary school crises will inevitably pull the head in one direction or the other. A disciplinary action against a student may provoke a completely irrational response in a parent, which makes it impossible for the head to maintain an empathic alliance with the family. A stupid mistake by a teacher may make it extremely difficult for the head to protect him or her, and the head's failure to stand behind the teacher can unnerve the faculty.

Achieving the ideal balance between parents and teachers is damnably difficult. What has been impressive to us is watching how many successful heads are able to do it. But it requires empathy, dexterity, political skill, and wisdom because—to go back to where we started this book—the inherent tensions in the parent-teacher relationship, coupled with the multiple factors that intensify these for both parents and schools, will always be there.

It is not a problem that can be permanently solved. But it *is* a rich and fascinating dynamic dilemma at the heart of school life.

About the Authors

Robert Evans, Ed.D., is a psychologist and school consultant. A former high school and preschool teacher and a former child and family therapist, he has consulted to more than 1,700 schools, including 700 NAIS schools. He served for nearly 40 years as executive director of the Human Relations Service, a nonprofit mental health agency in Wellesley, Massachusetts.

Evans' interests are in leadership, helping schools manage change, improving adult relationships within schools, and crisis intervention. He is the author of many articles and three books, including *Seven Secrets of the Savvy School Leader: A Guide to Surviving and Thriving* and *The Human Side of School Change*.

Evans is an independent school graduate, and his children and grandchildren have all attended independent schools.

Michael Thompson, Ph.D., is a clinical psychologist, author, and school consultant. He has worked in schools for 50 years, starting out as a middle school teacher and later training as a counselor and psychologist.

Now the supervising psychologist for the Belmont Hill School (MA), he has worked with more than 700 schools in the U.S., Asia, Africa, Europe, and Central America. In addition, he served as the longtime facilitator for the NAIS Institute for New Heads and later for the Academy of International School Heads. He has also served on the board of the American Camp Association.

Thompson is the author or coauthor of nine books, including the *New York Times* bestseller *Raising Cain: Protecting the Emotional Life of Boys* and *Best Friends, Worst Enemies: Understanding the Social Lives of Children*.

Like Evans, Thompson attended independent schools, as did his children and grandchildren.